THE MAILBOX®

The Education Center®

S0-AHG-678

Graphic Organizers

Over 50 Easy-to-Adapt Organizers That Help Students

- Make Predictions

- Compare and Contrast

- Explore Story Elements

- Summarize

- Sequence

- Collect Data

- Determine Cause and Effect

- Build Vocabulary

- Make Decisions

And Much, Much More!

Improve reading and writing skills!

Written by Elizabeth H. Lindsay

Editorial Team: Becky S. Andrews, Kimberley Bruck, Karen P. Shelton, Diane Badden, Thad H. McLaurin, Debra Liverman, Peggy Hambright, Karen A. Brudnak, Hope Rodgers, Dorothy C. McKinney

Production Team: Lisa K. Pitts, Pam Crane, Rebecca Saunders, David G. Bullard, Jennifer Tipton Cappoen, Chris Curry, Sarah Foreman, Theresa Lewis Goode, Clint Moore, Greg D. Rieves, Barry Slate, Donna K. Teal, Zane Williard, Tazmen Carlisle, Cat Collins, Marsha Heim, Amy Kirtley-Hill, Lynette Dickerson, Mark Rainey, Debbie Shoffner

www.themailbox.com

©2006 The Mailbox®
All rights reserved.
ISBN10 #1-56234-695-4 • ISBN13 #978-156234-695-9

Manufactured in the United States
10 9 8 7 6 5 4 3 2

Table of Contents

How to Use

1 Scan the table of contents to find just the right organizer to meet your objectives.

2 Read the accompanying teacher page for simple directions on how to complete the organizer and use it in several different curriculum areas.

3 Make copies of the organizer for your students.

Teacher Page

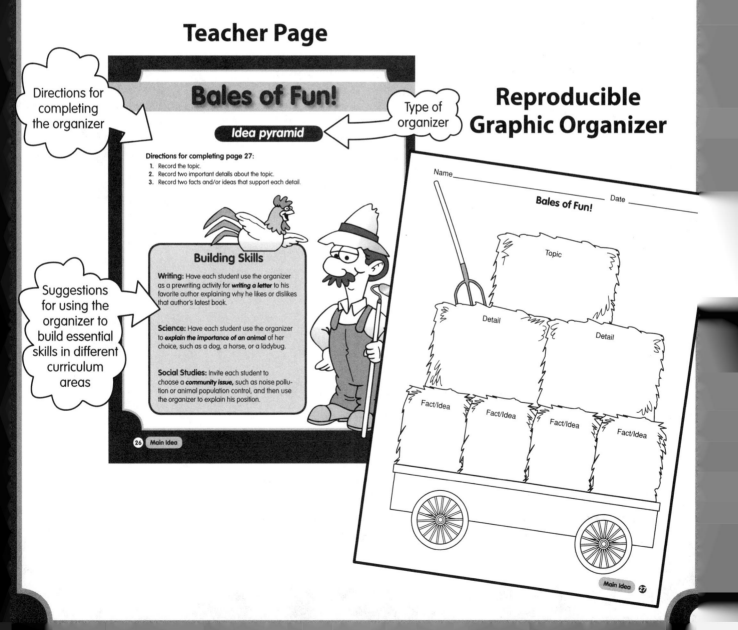

Directions for completing the organizer

Suggestions for using the organizer to build essential skills in different curriculum areas

Bales of Fun!

Idea pyramid

Type of organizer

Reproducible Graphic Organizer

Directions for completing page 27:
1. Record the topic.
2. Record two important details about the topic.
3. Record two facts and/or ideas that support each detail.

Building Skills

Writing: Have each student use the organizer as a prewriting activity for *writing a letter* to his favorite author explaining why he likes or dislikes that author's latest book.

Science: Have each student use the organizer to *explain the importance of an animal* of her choice, such as a dog, a horse, or a ladybug.

Social Studies: Invite each student to choose a *community issue*, such as noise pollution or animal population control, and then use the organizer to explain his position.

26 Main Idea

Name _____

Date _____

Bales of Fun!

Topic

Detail

Detail

Fact/Idea Fact/Idea Fact/Idea Fact/Idea

Main Idea 27

Premier Predictions

Prereading organizer

Directions for completing page 5:

1. Record the title. Then scan the title and any boldfaced headings to identify clues that may help you predict what the selection is about. Record your findings.
2. Scan any pictures for clues about the selection's topic. Record your findings.
3. Identify other clues, such as boldfaced vocabulary words. Record your findings.
4. Guided by the clues you've gathered, write in the box your prediction about the topic. After reading the selection, rate your prediction. Color one to four stars, with one star meaning your prediction was incorrect, two to three stars meaning your prediction needed adjusting, and four stars meaning your prediction was confirmed.

Building Skills

Reading: Show students a book jacket of a novel they will be reading. Have them use the organizer to detail predictions about the ***book's plot.*** Collect the organizers and redistribute them after reading the novel. Then have students rate their predictions.

Science/Social Studies: Assign each student a reading selection about a ***famous scientist or historic figure.*** Have him use the organizer to detail predictions about what the person is famous for. After reading the selection, have students rate their predictions.

Social Studies: Before reading a selection about a particular ***historical event,*** have student pairs use the organizer to make predictions about the event's importance. Have each duo share its prediction. After reading the selection, have partners rate and discuss their predictions.

Name_____ Date _____

Premier Predictions

Title _____

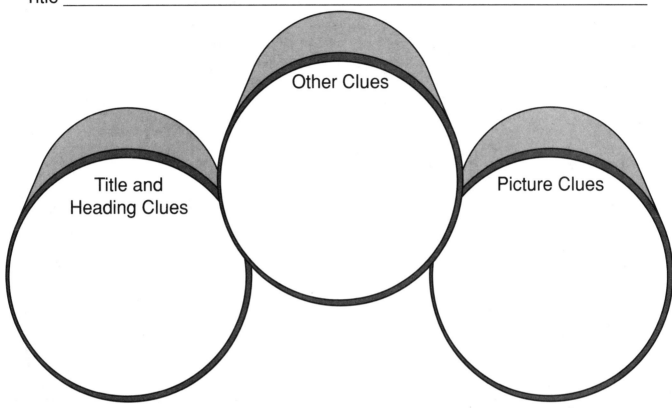

Other Clues

Title and
Heading Clues

Picture Clues

My prediction about the selection:

My prediction rating:

1 2 3 4

Piecing Together Predictions

Prediction chart

Directions for completing page 7:

1. Record the title on the thread line.
2. Scan the beginning of the selection and predict what you think it will be about. Write your prediction in the first column of the organizer. In the second column, record the clues that helped you make your prediction.
3. Read the beginning of the selection. In the third column of the organizer, write a sentence summarizing what you read.
4. In the organizer's last column, explain whether your prediction was correct.
5. Repeat Steps 2–4 to complete the organizer's middle and end sections.

Building Skills

Reading: Make a transparency of the organizer. Then have students help you complete it to **preview your next read-aloud novel.**

Reading: Have students use the organizer to **preview a sequel to a class novel** they've just read. Discuss whether having prior knowledge about the first book's characters and plot helped them make more accurate predictions about the sequel.

Social Studies: Give each small group of students a copy of the same **local current-events newspaper article.** Have the group use the organizer to predict what each section of the article is about. Have groups compare their predictions.

Name _____

Date _____

Piecing Together Predictions

Title: _____

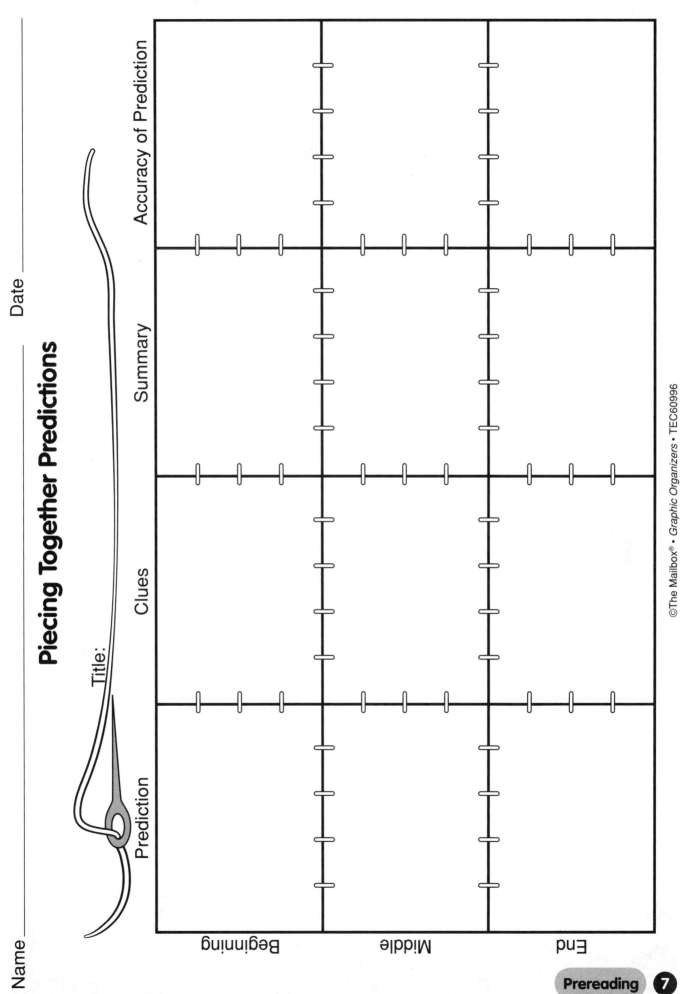

	Prediction	Clues	Summary	Accuracy of Prediction
Beginning				
Middle				
End				

In the Forecast

Forecasting chart

Directions for completing page 9:

1. Record the title.
2. Scan the beginning of the selection for clues about a problem that happens. In the first column of the organizer, write a sentence describing the problem.
3. In the "Forecast" column, record how you think the problem will be solved.
4. Read the beginning of the selection. Then explain in the "Outcome" column how the problem was solved.
5. Repeat Steps 2–4, identifying problems that occur in the middle and end of the selection.

Building Skills

Reading: Have students use the organizer to **make ongoing predictions** of how a particular character in a book they are reading will handle problems that occur throughout the text.

Social Studies: Before students read about a new state, region, or country, have them skim their textbooks or other reference books to get a feel for that area's climate, physical features, and population. Then tell students that they are going to take an imaginary vacation to this location. Have student pairs use the organizer to **detail potential problems and solutions** for the beginning, middle, and end of the trip; then have them read about the place to see whether problems they identified were valid.

Name _____

Date _____

In the Forecast

Title: _____

Problem	Forecast	Outcome
Beginning		
Middle		
End		

Cool Collection

KWL chart

Directions for completing page 11:

1. Record the topic.
2. Think about what you already know about the topic. Write your thoughts in the first jar.
3. Decide what you want to find out about the topic. List your questions in the second jar.
4. Read the selection to find the answers to your questions. Summarize in the third jar what you learned about the topic.

Building Skills

Reading: Before students read a selection, list its *unfamiliar or important vocabulary words* on the board. Assign each student pair a different word from the list and give the pair a copy of the organizer. Have the pair use the organizer's first two sections to detail what they know and want to know about the assigned word. Students then should refer to a dictionary to complete the last section.

Writing: As an extension activity, have each student use the information in the "What I Learned" section of the organizer to write a *news report, short story, or poem.*

Social Studies: Assign each student a *U.S. city, a U.S. state, or another country.* Have her use the organizer's first two sections to list what she knows and wants to know about the assigned city, state, or country. After she reads various resources to research the answers to her questions, she can use the last section of the organizer to detail her findings.

Name _____

Date _____

Cool Collection

Topic: _____

What I Know

What I Want to Know

What I Learned

Snapshots

Storyboard

Directions for completing page 13:

1. Record the title of the reading selection.

2. Identify two important events that occur at the beginning of the selection. Illustrate the event that happens first on snapshot 1 and the other event on snapshot 2. Write a caption below each illustration.

3. Repeat the process for the middle of the selection using snapshots 3 and 4 and for the end of the selection using snapshots 5 and 6.

4. Check your snapshots to make sure they show the correct chronological order.

Building Skills

Writing: Have each student use the organizer as a **prewriting activity** to help him sequence and summarize an important life event, such as learning to ride a bike, winning an award, or taking a special vacation.

Science: Use the organizer to **assess a student's grasp of a sequential process,** such as the life cycle of an animal or plant, the rock cycle, or the water cycle.

Social Studies: Have the student use the organizer to **retell a historical event in chronological order.**

Name _____

Date _____

Snapshots

Title: _____

3

2

6

5

1

4

Here's the Scoop!

Beginning, middle, end

Directions for completing page 15:

1. Record the title of the reading selection.

2. In the top scoop, describe the main event that happens in the beginning of the selection.

3. In the middle scoop, describe the main event that occurs in the middle of the selection.

4. In the bottom scoop, describe the main event that happens at the end of the selection.

5. Review your descriptions to make sure they show the correct chronological order.

Building Skills

Reading: Have students use the organizer as a *planning tool for an upcoming booktalk.* Direct each child to list on the organizer the important characters, setting, and plot introduced in the beginning, in the middle, and at the end of his book; then have him use the page as a guide when he presents the booktalk.

Writing: Have students use the organizer as a *prewriting activity* for describing the perfect school day from beginning to end.

Social Studies: Share with students a *historical journey,* such as the Cherokees' Trail of Tears or the Lewis and Clark expedition. Have each child use the organizer to summarize what happened in the beginning, in the middle, and at the end of the journey.

Here's the Scoop

Beginning

Middle

End

title

Roll 'Em!

Filmstrip organizer

Directions for completing page 17:

1. Record the title of the reading selection.
2. As you read, identify six important events that occur from beginning to end.
3. Illustrate each event in the appropriate filmstrip section.
4. Below each illustration, write a brief caption describing the event.

DIRECTOR

Building Skills

Any Subject Area: Have students use the organizer to help them prepare an *oral presentation*. Then allow each presenter to refer to his organizer as he speaks.

Math: Use the organizer to *assess a student's understanding* of a multistep math concept, such as multiplication of larger numbers or long division. Have the child write the problem in the first box and then use the remaining boxes to explain each successive step needed to complete the problem.

Science: Have students use the organizer to *plan the steps for a science experiment* or investigation. Then meet with the student about his plan and discuss any changes that may be needed before beginning the study.

Name _____

Date _____

Roll 'Em!

Title: _____

Scene 2
Take 20

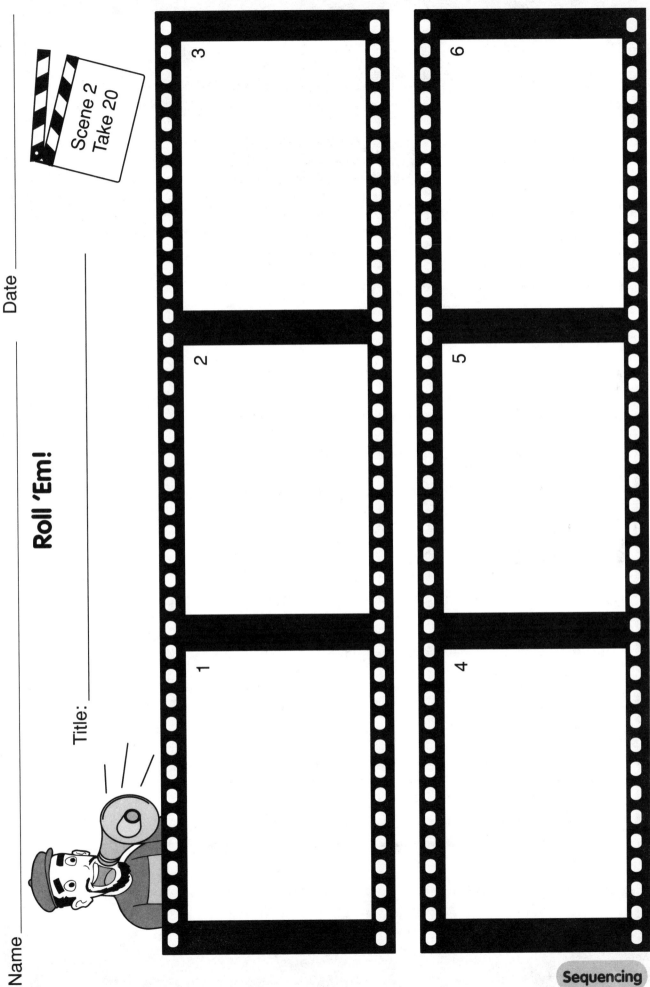

| 3 | 2 | 1 |
| 6 | 5 | 4 |

Lily Pad Leap

Flowchart

Directions for completing page 19:

1. Record the topic/title.
2. Choose five key events.
3. Describe each event in chronological order on the appropriate lily pad.

Building Skills

Writing: Have students use the lily pads to organize their thoughts for a **how-to paragraph.** Assign each child a different topic, such as caring for a pet, playing a particular sport, or making a particular food. Have writers list on the organizer the sequence of steps needed to complete the task and then refer to the page as they write their paragraphs.

Science: Have students use the organizer to explain the sequence of **a natural event,** such as the eruption of a volcano or the formation of a cloud.

Social Studies: During a **map skills** unit, have students use the organizer to explain the sequential steps of how to get from one area of the community to another. Encourage students to include cardinal directions.

Name _____ Date _____

Lily Pad Leap

Topic/Title: _____

First,

Next,

Then,

After that,

Finally,

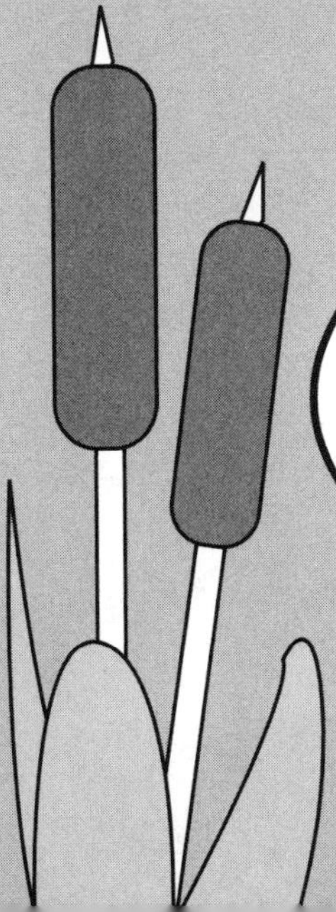

Round and Round We Go!

Directions for completing page 21:

1. Record the topic.
2. Think about the topic and its recurring cycle of events.
3. Record up to six of the events in chronological order on the Ferris wheel, beginning with the starred box.

Building Skills

Math: Have each student use the organizer to detail her **daily schedule,** beginning with waking in the morning and ending with going to bed at night. Direct her to record a time for each event at the top of the box. Then have her write a brief description of the event below the designated time.

Science: Have students use the organizer to explain a **cyclical process in nature,** such as the water cycle, the life cycle of a plant, or the circulation of blood throughout the body.

Social Studies: Assign each student pair a starting point somewhere on a globe. Have the partners use the organizer to identify locations needed to **travel around the world,** beginning and ending at the same point. Remind students that they can only make five stops along the way because the sixth stop returns them to the original starting point.

Round and Round We Go!

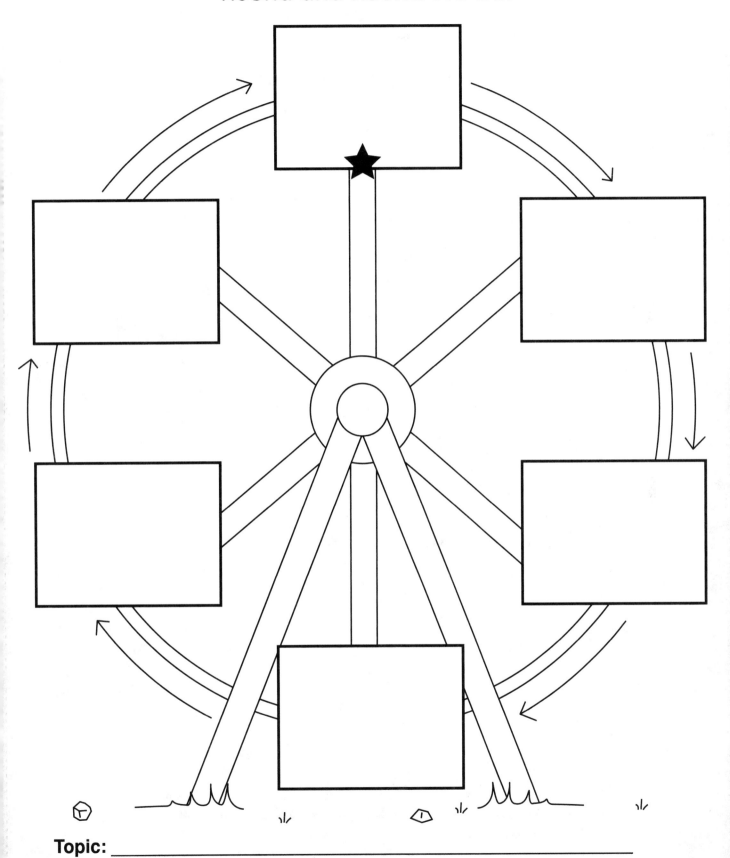

Topic: _____

T-Shirt Timeline

Timeline

Directions for completing page 23:

1. Record the title.
2. Identify up to eight important events that occur from beginning to end.
3. Record each event in chronological order on a separate T-shirt. Then write the date on the clothesline above the appropriate T-shirt.
4. Choose one event that you can connect to either your life, to someone else's life, or to a character from a story you've read. Explain the connection on the clothes basket.

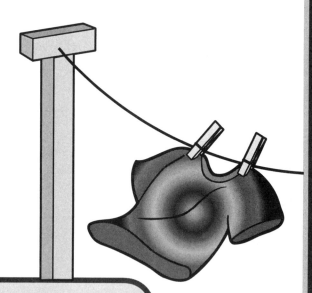

Building Skills

Writing: Have each student use the organizer as a prewriting activity for a **personal narrative** about a specific year in her life.

Social Studies: Assign each student a specific time period in our nation's history. Have the student use the organizer to detail **historical milestones** during that period.

Social Studies: Give each student a reading selection about a **notable person in history.** Have the child use the organizer to highlight important events in that person's life.

Name _____

T-Shirt Timeline

Title: _____

Dates: _____

Dates: _____

©The Mailbox® • *Graphic Organizers* • TEC60996

Bubbling With Ideas

Idea web

Directions for completing page 25:

1. Record the topic.
2. Record three important details about the topic.
3. For each detail, record two facts and/or ideas that support that detail.

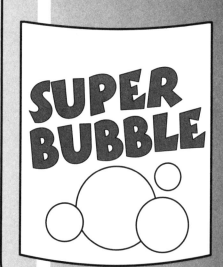

Building Skills

Writing: Have each student use the organizer as a prewriting activity for a *persuasive-writing* assignment.

Science/Social Studies: Have students use the organizer to *record information* gathered about an assigned research topic.

Social Studies: Assign each student pair a *current events issue* that people are either for or against. Give the partners two copies of the organizer to complete: one copy listing details and facts supporting the issue and another copy listing details and facts opposing the issue.

Name _____

Bubbling With Ideas

Fact/Idea

Fact/Idea

Fact/Idea

Fact/Idea

Fact/Idea

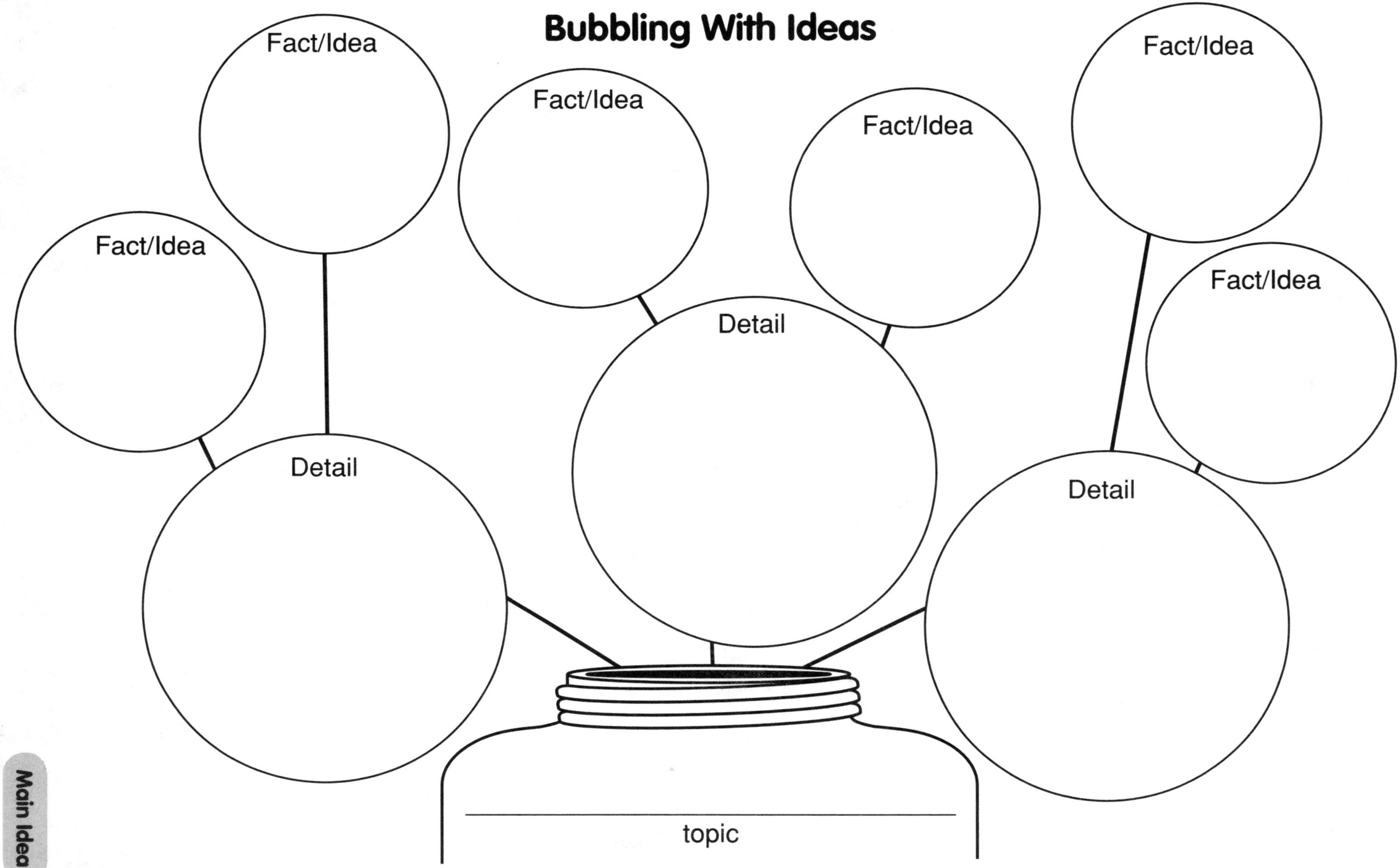

Fact/Idea

Fact/Idea

Detail

Detail

Detail

topic

Bales of Fun!

Directions for completing page 27:

1. Record the topic.
2. Record two important details about the topic.
3. Record two facts and/or ideas that support each detail.

Building Skills

Writing: Have each student use the organizer as a prewriting activity for **writing a letter** to his favorite author explaining why he likes or dislikes that author's latest book.

Science: Have each student use the organizer to **explain the importance of an animal** of her choice, such as a dog, a horse, or a ladybug.

Social Studies: Invite each student to choose a **community issue,** such as noise pollution or animal population control, and then use the organizer to explain his position.

Name _____ Date _____

Bales of Fun!

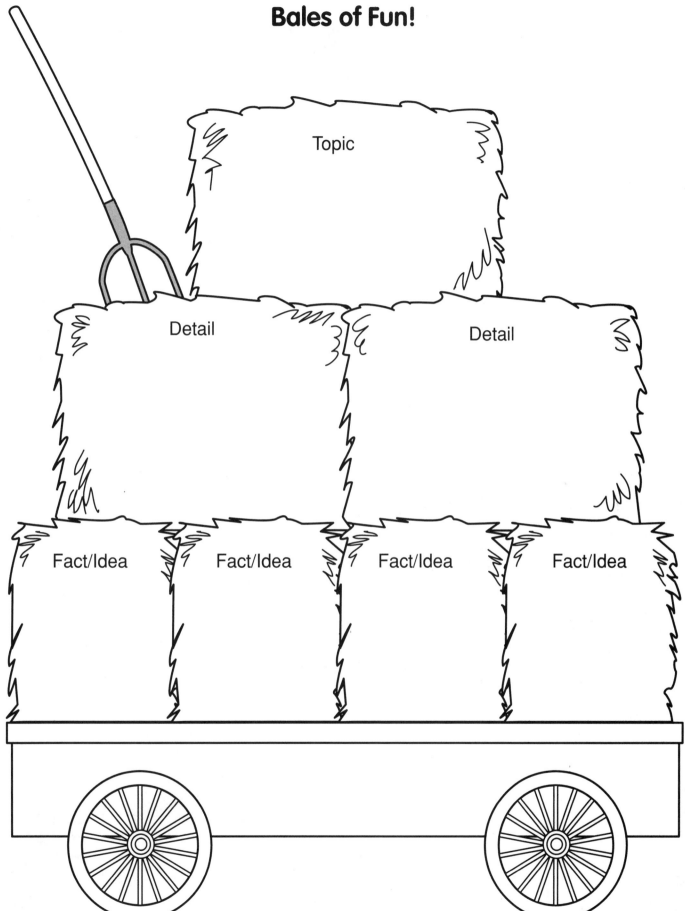

Topic

Detail

Detail

Fact/Idea

Fact/Idea

Fact/Idea

Fact/Idea

©The Mailbox® • *Graphic Organizers* • TEC60996

Main Idea 27

Sprouting With Ideas

Fishbone web

Directions for completing page 29:

1. Record the topic or title.
2. Write the main idea.
3. Identify six details related to the main idea. Write each detail on a separate leaf.

Building Skills

Reading: Have each student use the organizer to state and support **the main idea of a text** he is reading.

Science: Use a transparency of the organizer to help students summarize **the main idea of a science passage** from their textbooks or other science resource. Then have them skim the passage for details supporting the main idea. Record the details on the transparency.

Social Studies: Have student pairs each read a **news article** and then use the organizer to record the article's main idea and the details that support it.

Name_____ Date _____

Sprouting With Ideas

detail

detail

detail

detail

detail

detail

Main Idea:

_____
topic/title

Main Idea **29**

Give Me an E!

E chart

Directions for completing page 31:

1. Record the topic or title.
2. Write the main idea.
3. Record three details that support the main idea.

Building Skills

Reading: Use the organizer to **assess a student's comprehension** of a reading passage. After he reads the passage, have him record its topic (or title) and main idea; then have him list three details that support the main idea.

Writing: Have each student use the organizer as a prewriting activity **for creating a four-paragraph essay.** Direct the child to use the information he's listed in the "Main Idea" box to help him write the introductory paragraph. Instruct him to use the information in the three "Detail" boxes to write the three remaining paragraphs.

Name _____ Date _____

Give Me an E!

Topic/Title: _____

Detail:

Detail:

E

Detail:

Main Idea:

Main Idea **31**

Hanging on the Line

Summarizing chart

Directions for completing page 33:

1. Record the topic or title.
2. After reading a section or chapter, stop and think about what you've read.
3. On the first clothesline's sheet, write a one-sentence summary of the section.
4. Repeat Steps 2–3 for each remaining section, using clotheslines 2–5.

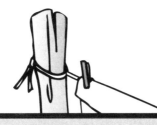

Building Skills

Math: Have a student use the organizer to summarize each step involved in solving a **math problem.**

Science: Have a student use the organizer to summarize the **steps of a science experiment or investigation.**

Social Studies: Use the organizer to help students summarize the **steps of the election process.**

Name_____ Date _____

Hanging on the Line

Topic/Title: _____

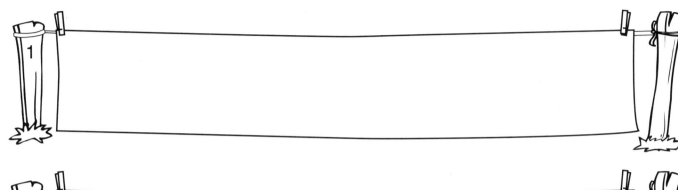

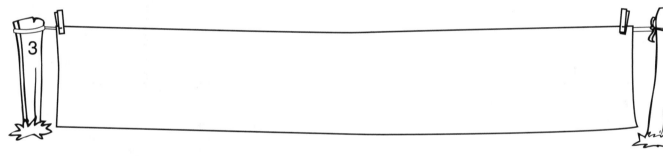

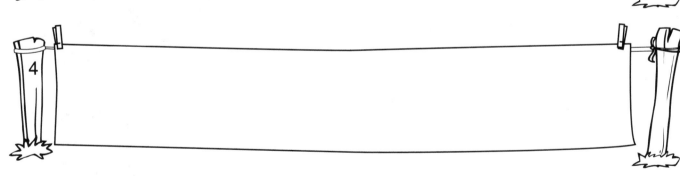

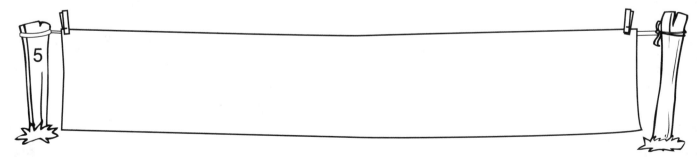

Music to My Ears

Story notes

Directions for completing page 35:
Record the title. As you read, record information about the story elements listed on the organizer.

Building Skills

Reading: Guide students to use the organizer as an *outline for booktalks.* Allow them to refer to it as they present their oral summaries.

Writing: Have each student use the organizer to *summarize his thoughts for an original story* about a favorite book character.

Social Studies: Have students use the organizer to *summarize information about an important historical event.*

Music to My Ears

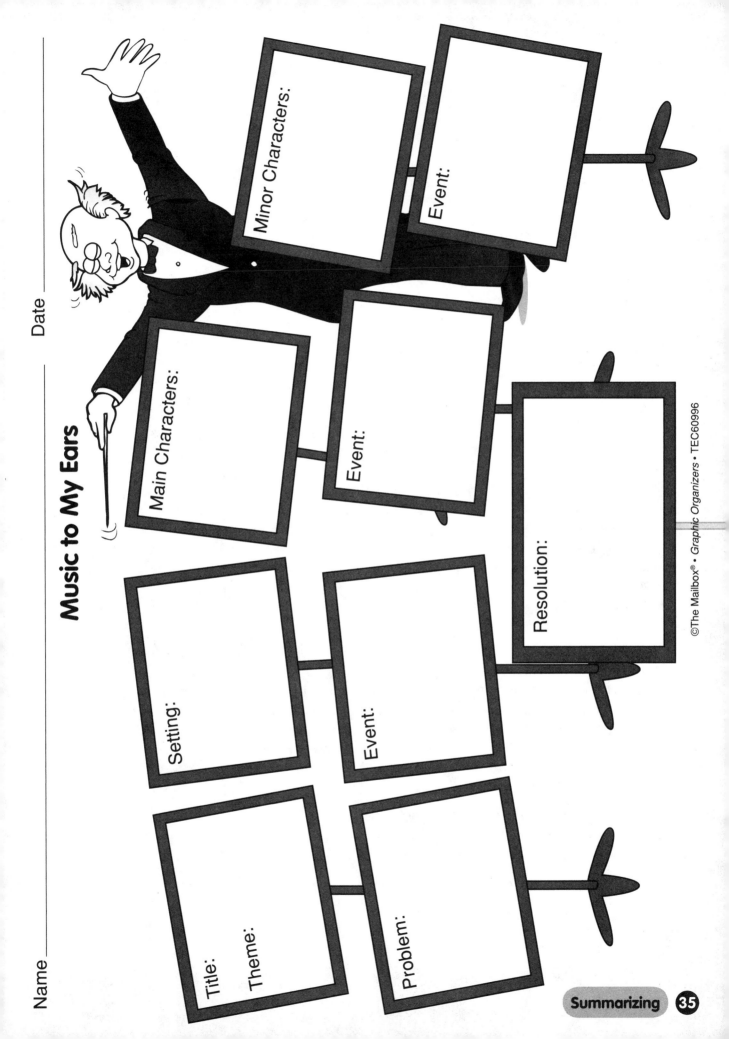

Main Characters:

Minor Characters:

Event:

Event:

Resolution:

Setting:

Event:

Title:

Theme:

Problem:

Out of This World!

Chapter map

Directions for completing page 37:

1. Record the title.
2. Record the chapter title and/or number.
3. As you read, think about four key events that occur in the chapter.
4. Write in the appropriate space a sentence to summarize each event.

Building Skills

Reading: Use the organizer to *assess a student's comprehension and summarizing skills* of a given chapter. Have him complete the organizer after he reads the selection. Then meet with the child and have him walk you through his chapter map.

Reading: Assign each student pair a different chapter of a book. Have the partners summarize the chapter by completing a chapter map and then illustrating on the back of the organizer a scene from the chapter. Compile the organizers in chronological order and bind them into a class book, providing a fun-to-read *class summary of an entire novel*.

Writing: Use the organizer to help each student *summarize a favorite trip* she's taken.

Name _____ Date _____

Out of This World!

First,

Chapter

_____

Finally,

Next,

Then,

Title: _____

You've Got Mail!

Who, what, when, where, why, and how chart

Directions for completing page 39:

1. Record the title.
2. Read the selection, looking for answers to the following questions: Who? What? When? Where? Why? How?
3. Record the answer to each question in the appropriate box.

Building Skills

Reading: Have a different student complete a copy of the organizer after each chapter of a current class novel has been read. Post each chapter's summary on a board. Students can use the board as a **quick way to review** what's happened in the book.

Writing: Have students use the organizer as a prewriting activity to create a **school or classroom news story.**

Writing/Social Studies: As a **quick assessment,** have each student use the organizer to summarize a historical event currently being studied.

Name _____

Date _____

You've Got Mail!

What?	**Where?**
Who?	**When?**
	How?
	Why?

Title: _____

A Masterpiece!

Directions for completing page 41:

1. Record the title and the character's name.
2. Write a different character trait at the bottom of each easel.
3. Skim the selection to find evidence that supports each trait. Record the evidence on the appropriate easel.

Building Skills

Reading: Provide each student in a group with a copy of the organizer. Have him complete the organizer for the main character in the novel the group is reading. Then have each student share his organizer. Have the group **analyze the character's traits.**

Writing: Have each student use the organizer as a prewriting activity for **developing a character** for an original creative-writing story.

Social Studies: Have students use the organizer to **describe the traits of a notable man or woman in history.**

Name _____

Date _____

A Masterpiece!

Title: _____

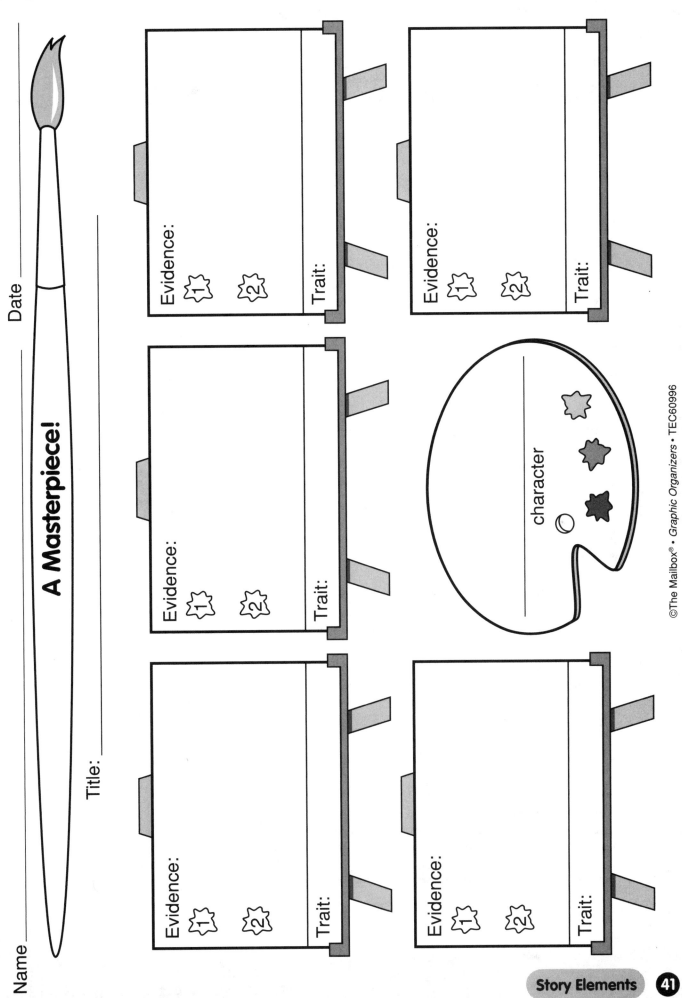

Evidence:
☆1
☆2
Trait: _____

Evidence:
☆1
☆2
Trait: _____

Evidence:
☆1
☆2
Trait: _____

Evidence:
☆1
☆2
Trait: _____

Evidence:
☆1
☆2
Trait: _____

character _____

A Door to Understanding

Character perspective chart

Directions for completing page 43:
1. Record the title and the character's name.
2. Write a brief description of an event from each section of the story.
3. Describe the character's point of view for each event.

Building Skills

Reading: Have students use the organizer to compare *two characters' points of view.* Have a pair of students complete one organizer for each character. Then have the students discuss whether the points of view of the two characters are similar or different.

Reading: Invite students to replace the character in a recent reading with a main character from another book, a television show, or a movie. Then have them use the organizer to retell the events from the *new character's point of view.*

Social Studies: Provide student pairs with two copies of the organizer. Then have the partners select two important people from the period of time being studied who were on *opposing sides.* Direct the students to complete one organizer for each key person to reveal two different points of view of the event.

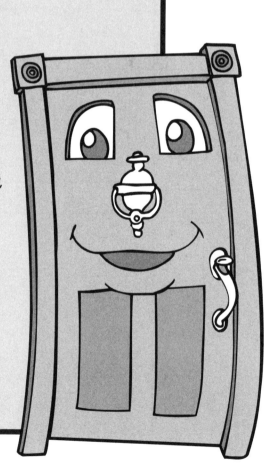

Name _____ Date _____

A Door to Understanding

Title: _____

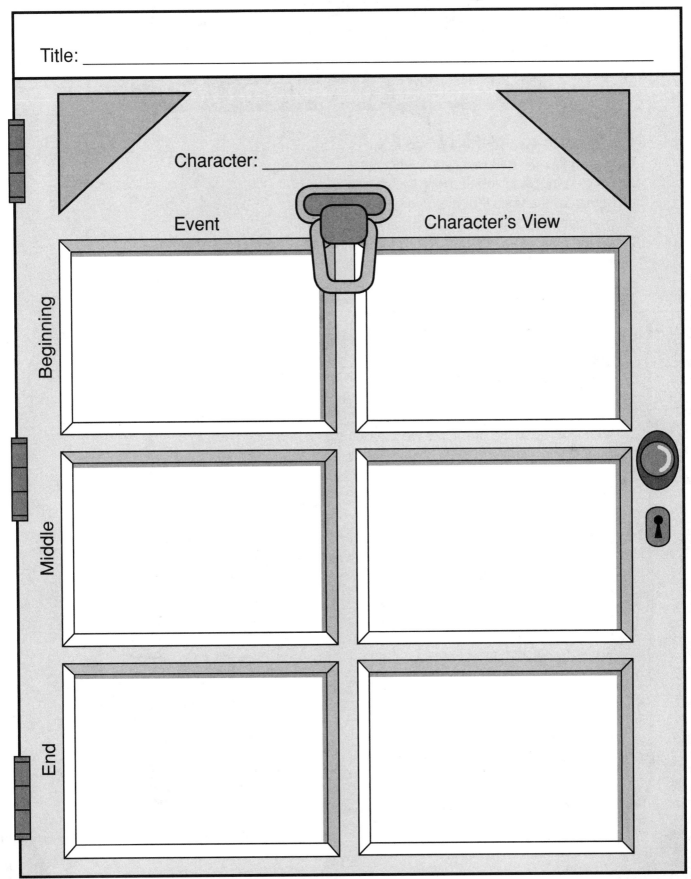

Character: _____

Event   Character's View

Beginning

Middle

End

Sighting Similarities

Character comparison chart

Directions for completing page 45:

1. Record the title and two characters' names.
2. On the binoculars labeled with a character's name, list the traits that are unique to that character.
3. On the binoculars labeled "Both Characters," list traits that both characters have in common.

Building Skills

Reading: Have students use the organizer to compare **characters from two different novels.**

Writing: Use the organizer with students as a prewriting activity to help them **develop two different characters** for an original story.

Social Studies: Have students use the organizer either to **compare two historical figures** from the same historical event or to compare two historical figures from two different periods of time, such as Abraham Lincoln and Dr. Martin Luther King Jr.

Sighting Similarities

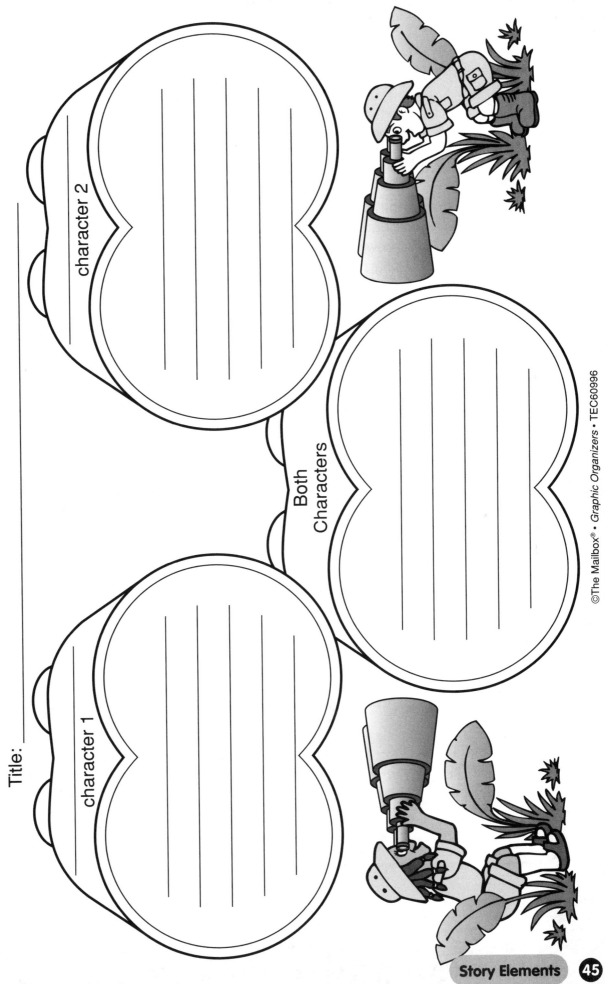

Title: _____

character 1

Both Characters

character 2

In Full Bloom

Personal connection web

Directions for completing page 47:
Record the title or topic and your name. On the appropriate petal, record how you personally connect or relate to the story's setting, the main character of the story, a problem from the story, and how that problem was resolved.

Building Skills

Language Arts: Have each student use the organizer to explain how he connects to the elements of a **recent movie** he's seen.

Social Studies: Read aloud a **current events article** from your local newspaper. Then have students use the organizer to relate their own personal experiences to the events that occurred in the article.

Social Studies: After students learn about a particular **historical event,** have them use the organizer to relate their own personal experiences to the event.

In Full Bloom

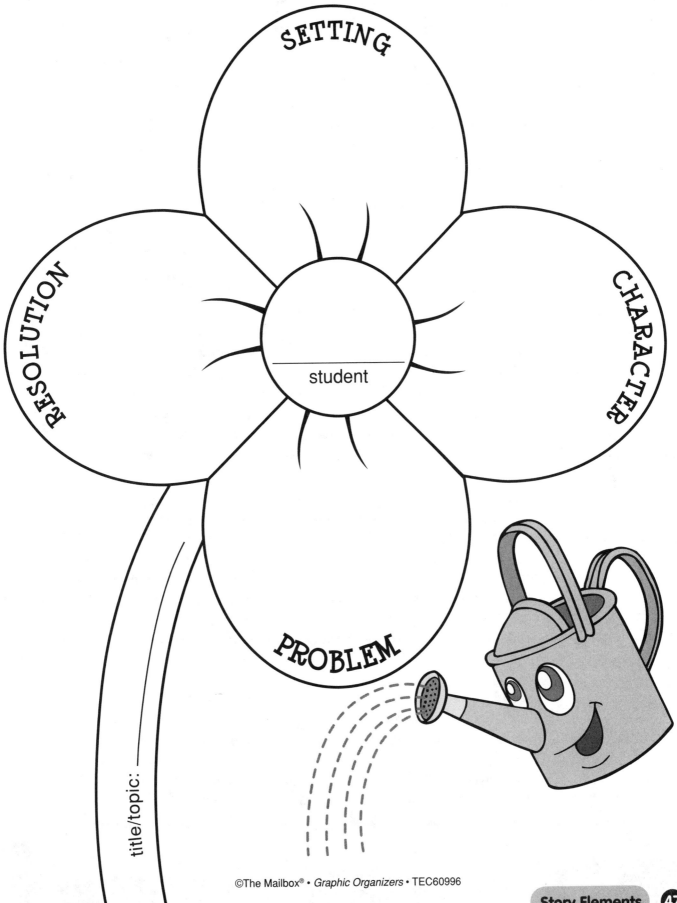

SETTING

RESOLUTION

CHARACTER

_____
student

PROBLEM

title/topic: _____

Building Relationships

Sociogram

Directions for completing page 49:

1. Record the title.
2. Record the main character's name in the center circle.
3. Record up to four different minor characters' names in the remaining circles.
4. On each line coming from the center circle, describe how the main character feels about the character to which the line is pointing.
5. On each line pointing to the center circle, describe how the minor character feels about the main character.
6. On the outer lines going to and from the outside circles, describe the relationships of the minor characters.

Building Skills

Reading: Have students complete an organizer at the middle of a book and again at the end of a book to **see how the characters' relationships change** during the course of the story.

Science: Program a copy of the organizer with the names of several plants and/or animals from an ecosystem your students are studying. Make a class set of the programmed organizer. Instruct students to use the organizer to describe the **relationships between the plants and animals** listed on the circles.

Social Studies: Have students use the organizer to describe the various **relationships between historical figures** during an important historical event. Brainstorm with your students a list of people involved in the event. Next, direct student pairs to write the name of the key or central figure of the event in the organizer's center circle and any four names from the list in the remaining circles. Then have the partners complete the organizer.

Building Relationships

Title:

Story Elements **49**

Up and Away!

Plot diagram

Directions for completing page 51:

1. Record the title.
2. Identify the main event at the beginning of the selection. Write details describing this event in the first balloon.
3. Repeat Step 2 for the remaining balloons to provide details about the middle of the selection, the climax (the turning point), and the conclusion.

Building Skills

Reading: Use the organizer to **assess a student's comprehension** of a story. After the student completes the organizer, meet with him and discuss his understanding of the plot.

Writing: Have each student complete an organizer as a prewriting activity for a **personal narrative about a significant event** in his life.

Writing: Have students use the organizer to plan the plot for an **original mystery or fantasy.**

Name _____

Up and Away!

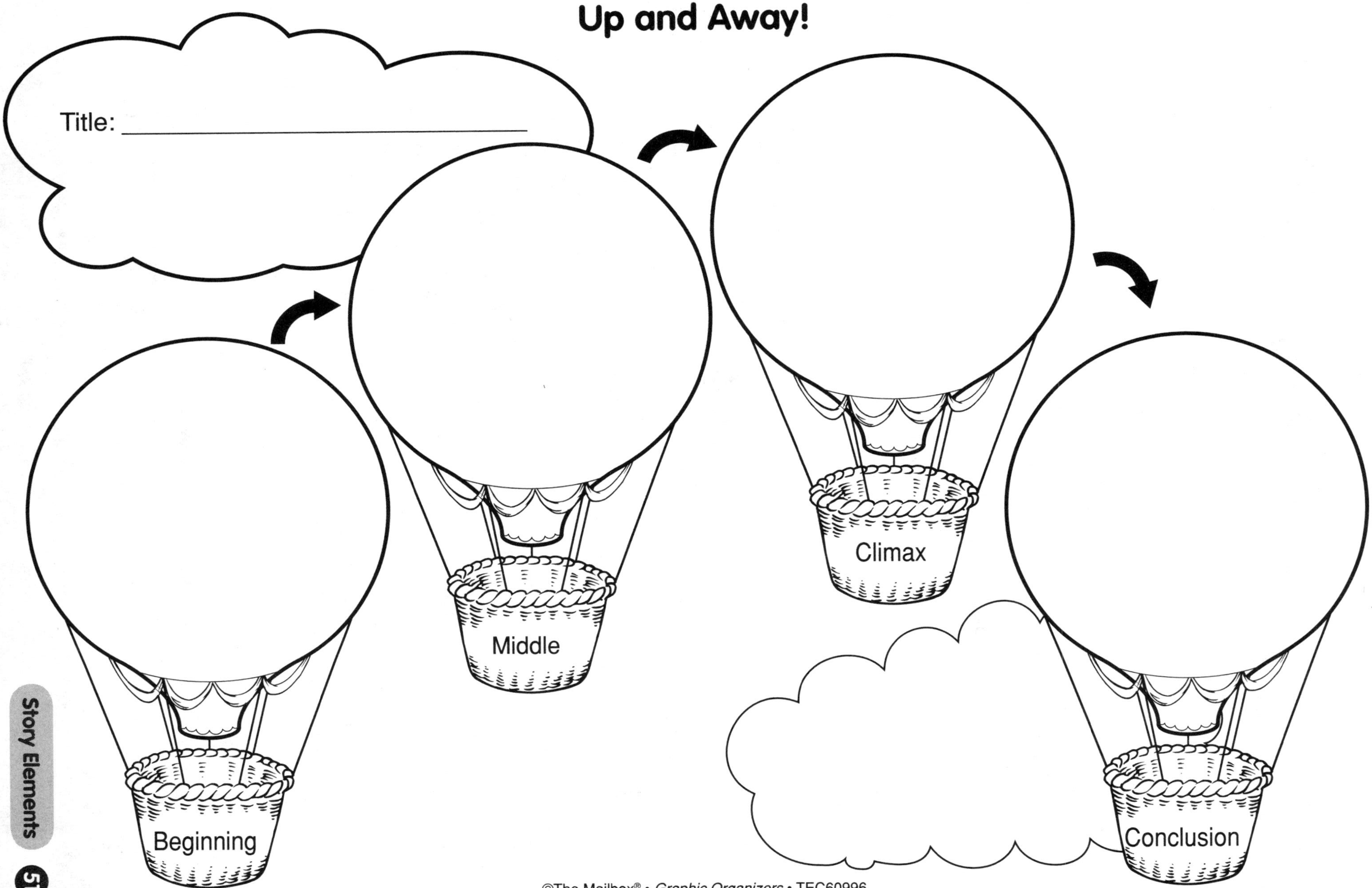

Title: _____

Beginning

Middle

Climax

Conclusion

Story Elements **51**

Story Wardrobe

Story map

Directions for completing page 53:

1. Record the title.
2. Record details about the setting and list the main characters.
3. Write a sentence to summarize the beginning, middle, and end of the story.

Building Skills

Reading: Have students use the organizer to **compare two works by the same author.** Have a student complete an organizer for each book. Then have him compare the two story maps and be prepared to discuss the similarities and differences between the two books.

Writing: Have students use the organizer to **plan a new version of a familiar fairy tale.**

Social Studies: Guide students to use the organizer to **summarize a news or magazine article.**

Name _____ Date _____

Story Wardrobe

Title: _____

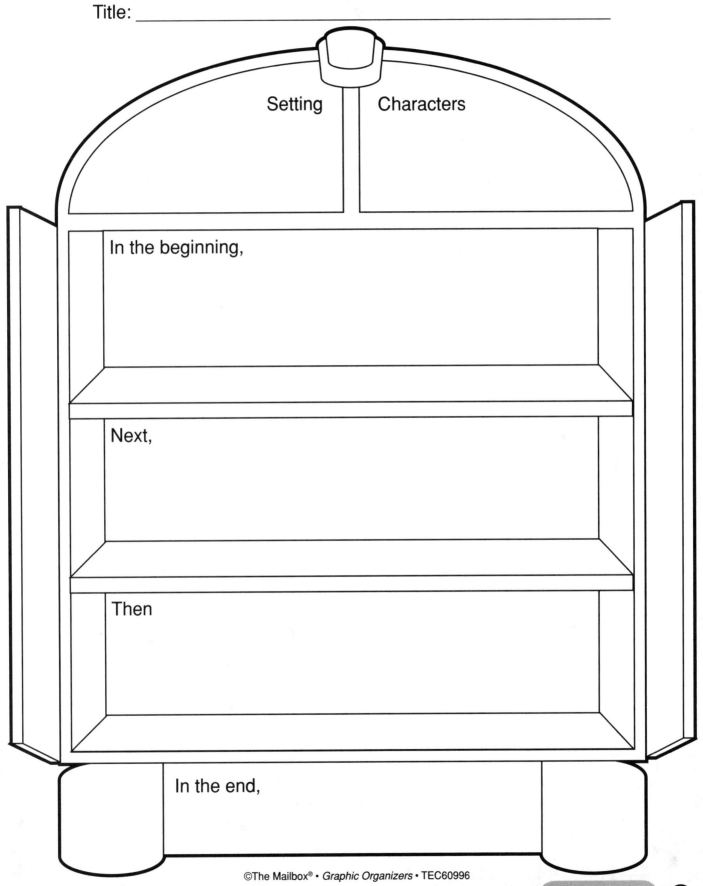

Setting   Characters

In the beginning,

Next,

Then

In the end,

Pack Your Bags!

Setting chart

Directions for completing page 55:

1. Record the title.
2. Describe the setting at the beginning of the selection. Include details that are important to the story.
3. Record the time of day for Setting 1. (It can be an approximate time such as morning, noon, or afternoon.)
4. Repeat Steps 2 and 3 for the middle and end of the story.
5. Explain the importance of time in one of the settings.

Building Skills

Reading: Provide student pairs with two copies of the organizer to use to **compare the settings of two different novels.**

Reading/Writing: Have students **change the time of each setting** and then write a brief description of the impact this time change may have on the story.

Name _____

Date _____

Pack Your Bags!

Title: _____

Setting 3 (End)

Time of Day: _____

Setting 2 (Middle)

Time of Day: _____

Setting 1 (Beginning)

Time of Day: _____

Choose one setting and explain the importance of time in that setting.

Get in Gear!

Problem-and-solution diagram

Directions for completing page 57:
1. Record the title or topic.
2. Describe a problem in the selection.
3. List evidence that the problem exists.
4. Describe how the problem was solved.
5. Tell what happened as a result of the solution. Tell whether the solution really solved the problem.

Building Skills

Reading: Once students identify a problem in a selection, have them complete the organizer's upper two gears. Before they read further, have them **brainstorm possible solutions** to the problem. Have each reader record the possible solutions and results on his organizer. Then, after the solution has been revealed, have students discuss the suggested solutions and whether they would have worked better or worse than the actual solution.

Science: Have students use the organizer to describe a **new invention** and the problem it could solve.

Social Studies: Have students use the organizer to **plan a solution** to a problem faced by the communities in which they live.

Name _____ Date _____

Get in Gear!

Title/Topic: _____

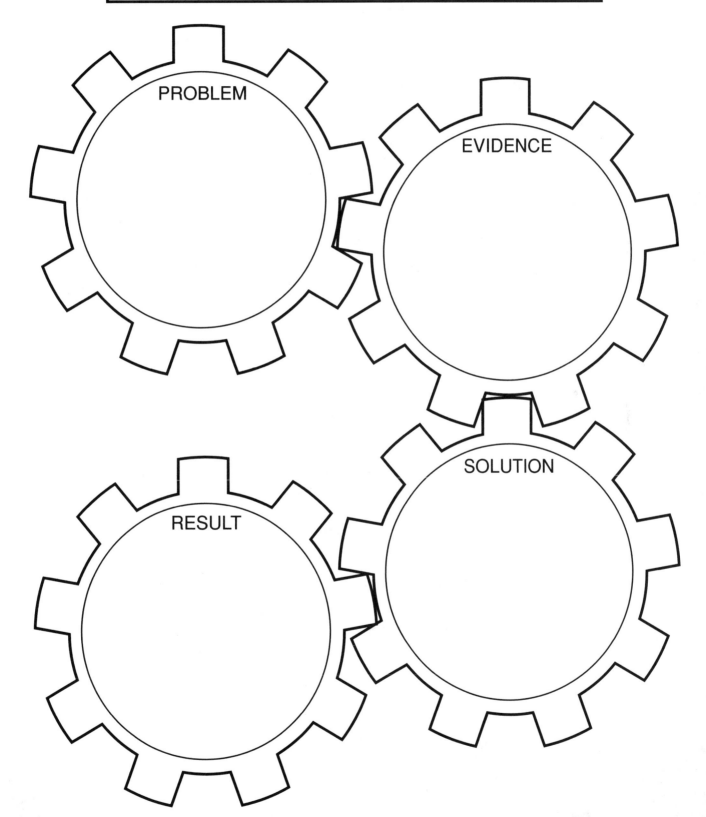

PROBLEM

EVIDENCE

RESULT

SOLUTION

Star Power!

Directions for completing page 59:

1. Record the title.
2. Preview the selection's headings, chapter names, and pictures for clues about the theme. Record your findings. Based on the clues, write your prediction on the star.
3. As you read the selection, record evidence that supports your prediction.
4. If the actual theme is different from the one you predicted, record it in the space provided.

Building Skills

Reading: *Introduce a new novel* by having student pairs complete the organizer. Collect the completed organizers. Halfway through the book, return the organizers and allow students to revise their predictions. Collect the organizers once again. Then, at the end of the book, return the organizers so students can discuss the accuracy of their predictions.

Reading: In advance, make a transparency of the organizer and program it with inaccurate predictions. Display the transparency; have **students evaluate your predictions** and determine whether you've done a good job.

Name _____

Date _____

Star Power!

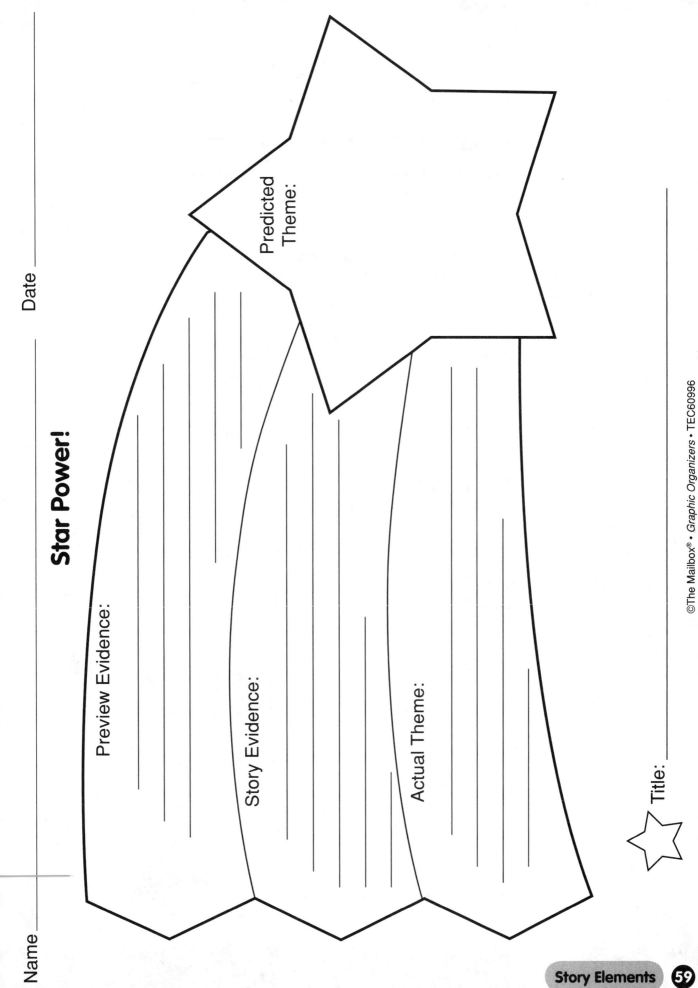

Predicted Theme:

Preview Evidence:

Story Evidence:

Actual Theme:

Title: _____

Brush It On!

Cause-and-effect chart

Directions for completing page 61:

1. Record the topic or title.
2. Identify a cause-and-effect relationship and write a brief description of the cause on the first paint can.
3. Describe the effect of that cause in the paint spill to the right of the can.
4. Repeat Steps 2 and 3 for two more cause-and-effect relationships in the selection.

Note: Sometimes it's easier for students to write the effect first and then describe the cause.

Building Skills

Reading: In advance, list on a transparency of the organizer up to three different causes students will encounter in a selection. Before they begin reading, display the transparency and discuss each cause. Have students **predict the effect** each cause will have. Record their predictions on the organizer. After reading the selection, revisit the students' predictions and discuss their accuracy.

Science: Have students use the organizer to identify a **cause and an effect of three different inventions,** such as the television, the cell phone, and the airplane.

Social Studies: Have students use the organizer to detail a **cause and an effect of three major historical events.** The events can all be related to the same historical period or can each be from a different period of time.

Name _____ Date _____

Brush It On!

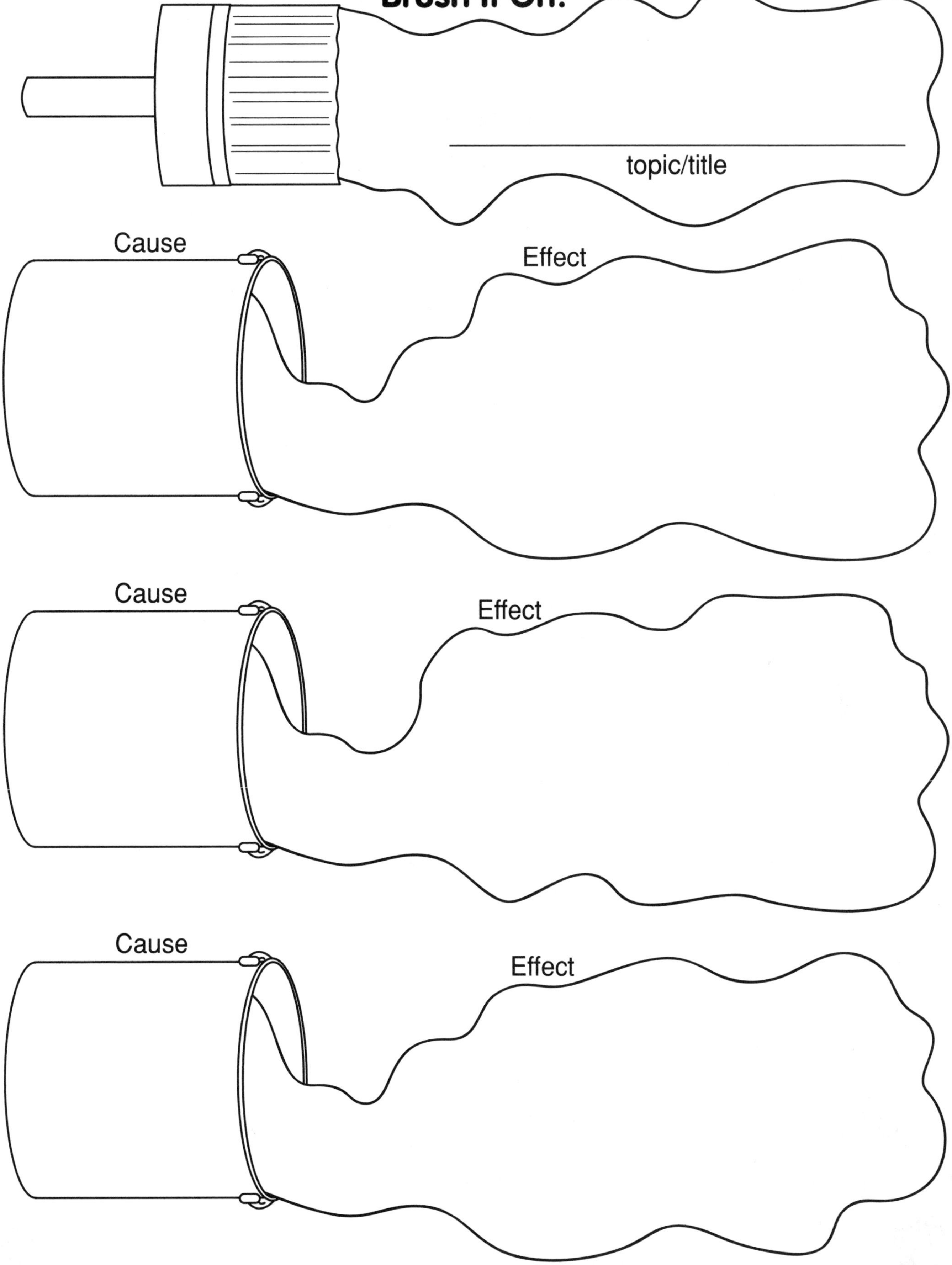

_____
topic/title

Cause

Effect

Cause

Effect

Cause

Effect

Cause and Effect **61**

Explosive Events

Chain of events chart

Directions for completing page 63:
1. Record the topic or title.
2. Identify up to four related events from the selection.
3. On each firecracker, write details that describe each sequential event.

Building Skills

Reading: As a *culminating activity and quick review of cause and effect* in a novel just read, have student pairs each complete an organizer for a different chapter of the book.

Writing: Have each student think of an event in his life. Next, have him use the organizer to summarize the cause(s) and effect(s) of the event. Then have the student use his summary to write a *personal narrative.*

Social Studies: Have students use the organizer to detail the *cause(s) and effect(s) of an important historical event,* such as the Boston Tea Party or Paul Revere's ride.

Name_____   Date _____

Explosive Events

Topic/Title: _____

KABOOM!

1 First, this happened.
_____
_____
_____
_____

2 This caused
_____
_____
_____
_____

3 That led to
_____
_____
_____
_____

POW!

4 This resulted in
_____
_____
_____
_____

BAM!

Makin' Tracks

Flowchart

Directions for completing page 65:

1. Record the topic or title.
2. As you read, think about the series of events taking place in the story.
3. In the spaces provided, describe up to six events in chronological order.

Building Skills

Reading/Writing: Have student pairs use the organizer to list the causes and effects of the event featured in a *news article.*

Math: Have each student use the organizer to explain the steps in solving *a real-life math problem,* such as determining sales tax or calculating the cost of a party.

Science: Use the organizer to help students explain the cause-and-effect relationship of a *science-related process,* such as how sound travels, how a rainbow is formed, or how blood travels to and from the heart.

Name_____ Date _____

Makin' Tracks

Topic/Title: _____

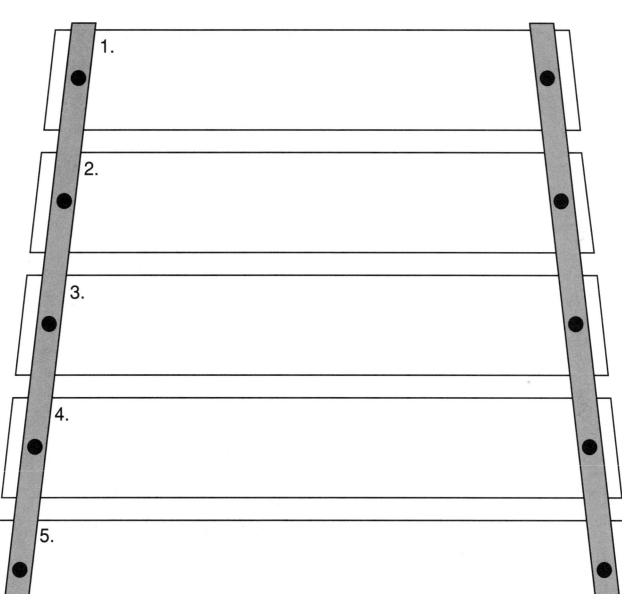

1.

2.

3.

4.

5.

6.

High-Flying Comparisons

Compare-and-contrast organizer

Directions for completing page 67:

1. Record the names of the two items being compared.
2. Record similarities (qualities both items have in common).
3. Record differences (qualities unique to each item).

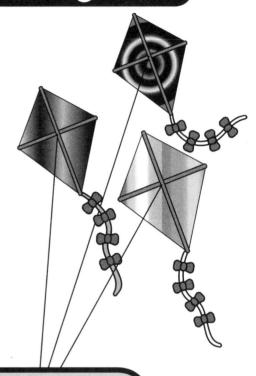

Building Skills

Reading: Have students use the organizer to compare **two different traditional tales** such as a tall tale and a fairy tale.

Reading: Have students use the organizer to compare **the protagonist (the main character) and the antagonist (the main character's opponent)** in a story.

Science: Use the organizer to help students compare **two different types of animals,** such as vertebrates and invertebrates.

Name_____ Date _____

High-Flying Comparisons

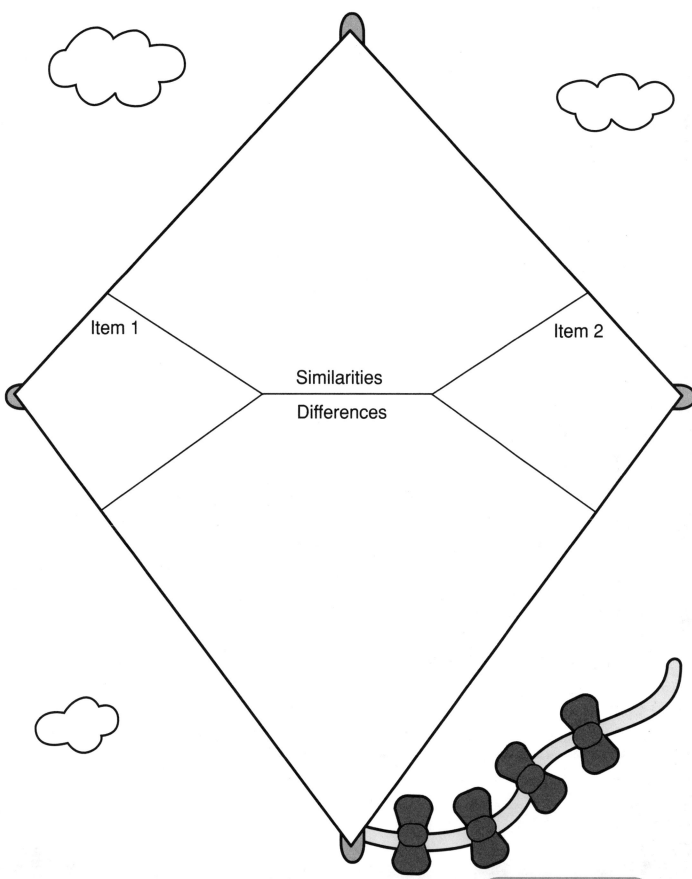

Item 1

Item 2

Similarities

Differences

Filing Away Comparisons

Comparison map

Directions for completing page 69:

1. Record the title or topic.
2. Write two settings, two characters' names, and two events on the appropriate file cabinet drawers.
3. On the corresponding file folders, write details telling how the settings, characters, and events are alike and different.

Building Skills

Reading: Have students use the organizer to compare and contrast settings, characters, and events within the **same book or two different books.**

Reading: Have students use the organizer to compare and contrast **two different versions of the same fairy tale.**

Social Studies: Use the organizer with students to help them compare and contrast the **environment, people, and activities of two different cultures.**

Name

Date

Filing Away Comparisons

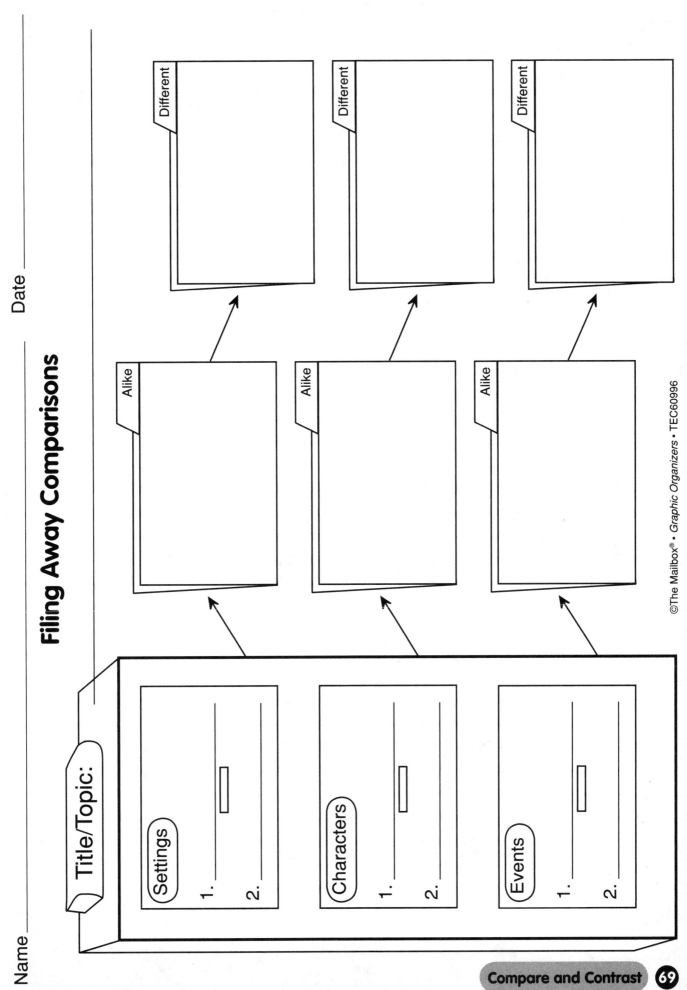

Title/Topic:

Settings
1.
2.

Characters
1.
2.

Events
1.
2.

Alike

Alike

Alike

Different

Different

Different

©The Mailbox® • *Graphic Organizers* • TEC60996

Wise Comparisons

Venn diagram

Directions for completing page 71:

1. Record the topic or title.
2. Record the two subjects (people, places, or things) being compared.
3. In the outer part of each eye, record details that are unique to that subject.
4. In the overlapping part of the eyes, record details about things the two subjects have in common.

Building Skills

Math: Have students use the organizer to compare two different *solid figures,* such as a cube and a rectangular prism.

Science: Have students use the organizer to compare and contrast two different *forms of energy,* such as kinetic and potential.

Social Studies: Use the organizer with students to help them compare two *colonies or two national documents.*

Name _____

Date _____

Wise Comparisons

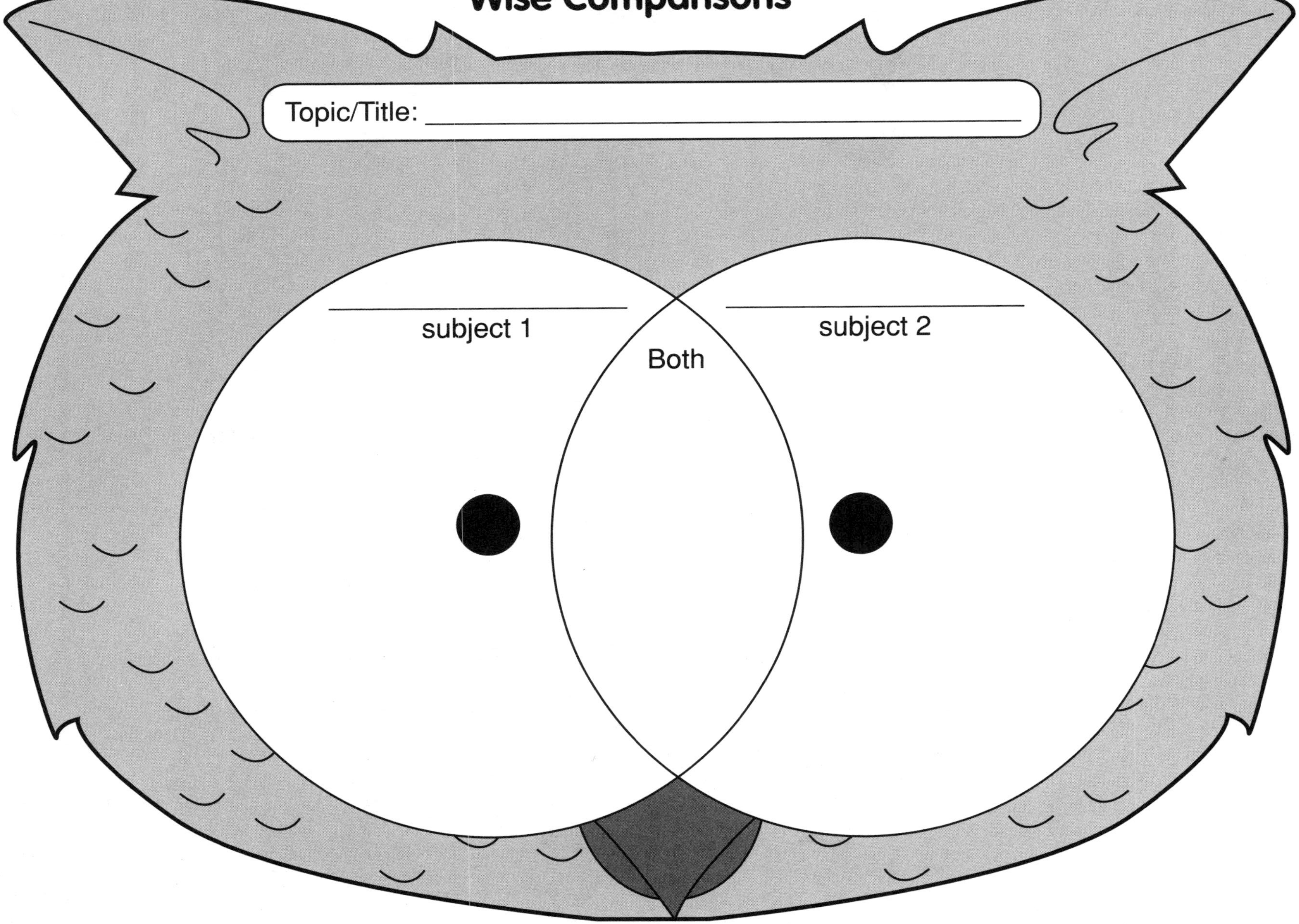

Topic/Title: _____

subject 2

Both

subject 1

Dish It Up!

Triple Venn diagram

Directions for completing page 73:

1. Record the topic or title.
2. Record the three subjects (people, places, or things) being compared.
3. On the outer section of each scoop, record details that are unique to that subject.
4. Where two scoops overlap, record details that those two subjects have in common.
5. In the center, where all three scoops overlap, record details that all three subjects have in common.

Building Skills

Reading: Have students use the organizer to compare *the settings of three different stories.*

Reading: Use the organizer to help students compare and contrast *three main characters* from different books.

Social Studies: Use the organizer with students to help them compare and contrast the *three branches of the federal government*—executive, legislative, and judicial.

Name _____ Date _____

Dish it Up!

Topic/Title: _____

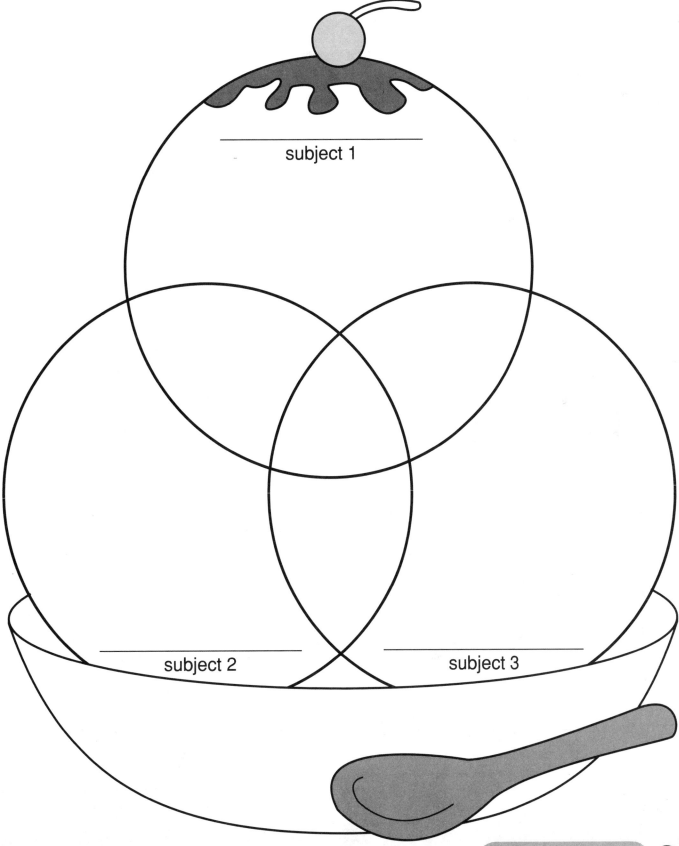

subject 1

subject 2

subject 3

Feel the Power!

T chart

Directions for completing page 75:

1. Record the topic or title.
2. Record the two subjects (people, places, or things) being compared.
3. Under subject 1, list details that are unique to that subject. Then do the same for subject 2.
4. Record similarities (things the two subjects have in common).

Building Skills

Reading: Have students use the organizer to compare and contrast **the plots of two books.**

Science: Have students use the organizer to compare and contrast **two planets.**

Social Studies: Use the organizer to help students compare and contrast **a map and a globe.**

Feel the Power!

Topic/Title: _____

_____   _____
subject 1   subject 2

(Similarities)

A Garden of Great Comparisons

H chart

Directions for completing page 77:

1. Record the topic or title.
2. Record the two subjects (people, places, or things) being compared.
3. Under subject 1, list details that are unique to that subject. Then do the same for subject 2.
4. Record similarities (things the two subjects have in common).

Building Skills

Reading: Have students use the organizer to compare *a fiction and a nonfiction selection.*

Science: Have students use the organizer to compare and contrast *two different types of animals,* such as mammals and birds.

Social Studies: Use the organizer to help students compare and contrast *two customs or traditions* within one culture or between two different cultures.

Name_____ Date _____

A Garden of Great Comparisons

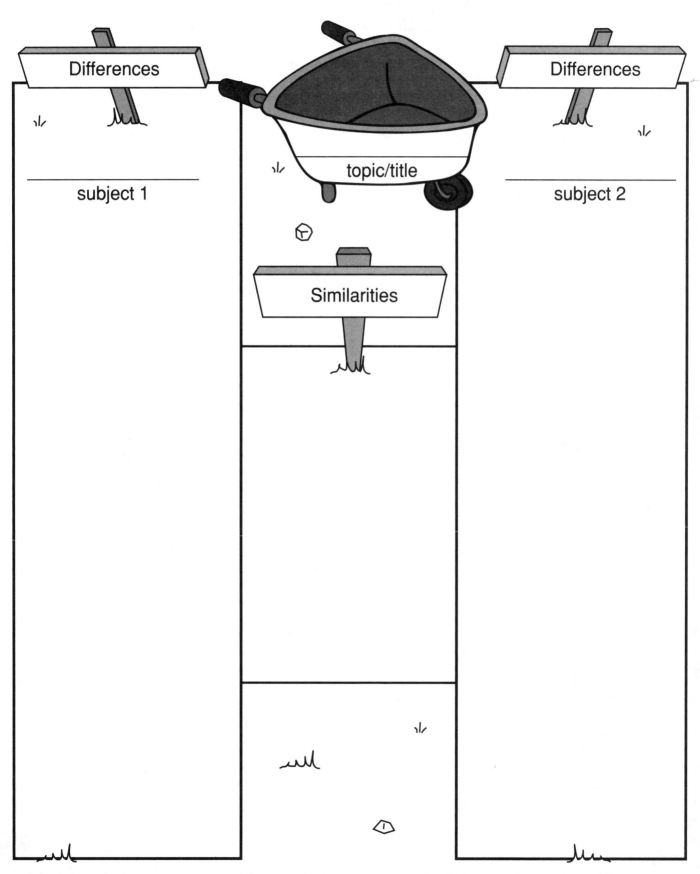

Differences

subject 1

topic/title

Differences

subject 2

Similarities

Movie Night

Word chart

Directions for completing page 79:

1. Write the vocabulary word.
2. Use context clues or a dictionary to help you define the word.
3. Use the word in a sentence to show its meaning.
4. Draw an illustration depicting the meaning of the word.
5. Use a thesaurus to help you create a list of antonyms and synonyms for the word.

Building Skills

Reading: Staple several copies of the organizer into a booklet for each child. Have the student use her booklet to record any challenging **multiple-meaning words** that she comes across in her reading.

Language Arts: To reinforce the spelling and understanding of **difficult weekly spelling words,** have a student complete an organizer for the selected words.

Science/Social Studies: Introduce new **science or social studies vocabulary words** by having student pairs complete an organizer for each word.

Name _____

Date _____

Movie Night

Synonyms

Antonyms

word _____

Definition:

Sentence:

Illustration:

Downstream

Word log

Directions for completing page 81:

1. Write the title.
2. Write a vocabulary word on each log.
3. Record the page number where each word is found.
4. Use the context of the word and/or a dictionary to define each word.

Building Skills

Reading: Have a student use a copy of the organizer to record and define **unfamiliar words** as she reads. Periodically have students share with the class some of the new words they've learned.

Science/Social Studies: Have each student use the organizer to record and define **unfamiliar terms** as he reads his textbook, news articles, or other informational sources.

Name_____ Date _____

Downstream

Title: _____

Word: _____

Page: _____

Definition:

Word: _____

Page: _____

Definition:

Word: _____

Page: _____

Definition:

Word: _____

Page: _____

Definition:

On the Case

Context clue chart

Directions for completing page 83:

1. Write each unfamiliar word and the page number on which it is found.
2. Record the context clues in the sentence and/or paragraph in which the word is found. Also write the clues in the word itself, such as its prefix, suffix, or root word.
3. Use the clues in Step 2 to guess the word's meaning. Record your guess.
4. Use a dictionary, an encyclopedia, a thesaurus, or another reference book to check your guess. If your guess is correct, put a check mark in the definition box. If your guess is not correct, record the actual definition in the box.

Building Skills

Reading: Have students complete the organizer for each chapter in a novel they are reading, recording up to four **unfamiliar words** per chapter.

Science/Social Studies: In advance, program a copy of the organizer with four **key science or social studies words** from an upcoming unit. When introducing the unit, give a copy of the programmed organizer to each student. As readers come upon each word in the text, have them fill in the organizer's remaining sections.

Name _____

Date _____

On the Case

Word	Context Clues	My Guess	Definition
Page ___			
Page ___			
Page ___			
Page ___			

©The Mailbox® • Graphic Organizers • TEC60996

Colorful Language

Figurative language chart

Directions for completing page 85:
1. Record the title.
2. On each crayon, record both a sentence that contains one of the four listed types of figurative language and the page number on which that sentence is found.
3. Explain the meaning of the sentence.
4. Check the box that tells what type of figurative language the example represents.

Building Skills

Reading: Have students use the organizer to go on a **simile or metaphor hunt.** Assign students a particular chapter in the novel they are reading. Then direct each child to see how many examples he can find.

Reading: Use the organizer to review the **different types of figurative language.** Assign each group of three or four students one type of figurative language: simile, metaphor, personification, or hyperbole. Then have the group members scan the reading selection and record their findings on the organizer.

Reading: Have students use the organizer to record examples of figurative language found in different **types of poetry,** such as free verse, limerick, haiku, and cinquain.

Name _____ Date _____

Colorful Language

Title: _____

Sentence from text:

Meaning:

Simile ☐ Metaphor ☐ Personification ☐ Hyperbole ☐

Page _____

Sentence from text:

Meaning:

Simile ☐ Metaphor ☐ Personification ☐ Hyperbole ☐

Page _____

Sentence from text:

Meaning:

Simile ☐ Metaphor ☐ Personification ☐ Hyperbole ☐

Page _____

Sentence from text:

Meaning:

Simile ☐ Metaphor ☐ Personification ☐ Hyperbole ☐

Page _____

Getting the Facts

Question-and-answer chart

Directions for completing page 87:
1. Record the title or topic.
2. Before reading, record in the organizer's left column several questions you have about the story or topic. Then, as you read, add other questions that come to mind.
3. As the answers to your questions are revealed, record them in the right column of the organizer.

Building Skills

Reading: Have students use the organizer at the **halfway point of a novel** to jot down any questions they have about the plot, the setting, or particular characters. After completing the book, have students revisit their organizers to see how many of their questions they can now answer.

Science: Have each student use the organizer to list questions he has prior to beginning a **science fair project.** Then meet with the student and allow him to pose each question.

Social Studies: Have students use the organizer to plan a series of **interview questions** to ask a staff member, family member, or significant member of the community.

Name_____ Date _____

Getting the Facts

Title/Topic: _____

<u>Question</u>	<u>Answer</u>

Rise and Shine!

KWS chart

Directions for completing page 89:
1. Record the topic.
2. Write what you know about the topic.
3. List questions you have or things you want to learn about the topic.
4. Record possible sources where the answers to your questions could be found.

Building Skills

Reading: Sometimes while reading a novel, students become interested in a *topic or hobby* that's mentioned in the story. Have students use the organizer to further explore this newfound interest.

Science: Have each student use the organizer as a *planning tool* for an upcoming science project.

Social Studies: Before *beginning a new social studies unit,* have students complete the first section of the organizer to get a feel for how much they already know about the topic. Then discuss with students what questions they have about the unit and where they may be able to find the answers.

Name _____

Rise and Shine!

Possible **Sources**

What I **Want** to Know

topic

What I **Know**

©The Mailbox® • *Graphic Organizers* • TEC60996

Bowl-a-rama

SQ3R chart

Directions for completing page 91:

1. Record the topic.
2. **Survey:** Preview the selection and record the title, subtitles, and any words or phrases written in special type. Make notes about any illustrations, charts, diagrams, end-of-unit summaries, or questions.
3. **Question:** Write who, what, when, where, and/or why questions about the topic.
4. **Read:** Read to find the answer to each question; take notes about the main idea.
5. **Recite:** Take time at the end of a paragraph, chapter, or section to orally answer questions. Jot down any key facts or phrases about each question.
6. **Review:** For this step, turn the organizer over and write a one-sentence summary for each question to use as a reference or study guide.

Building Skills

Reading: Have students use the organizer to do an in-depth study of a key chapter in a **nonfiction book.**

Science/Social Studies: Have students use the organizer before, during, and after reading a unit in their **textbooks or other informational books.**

Name _____

Bowl-a-rama

Question

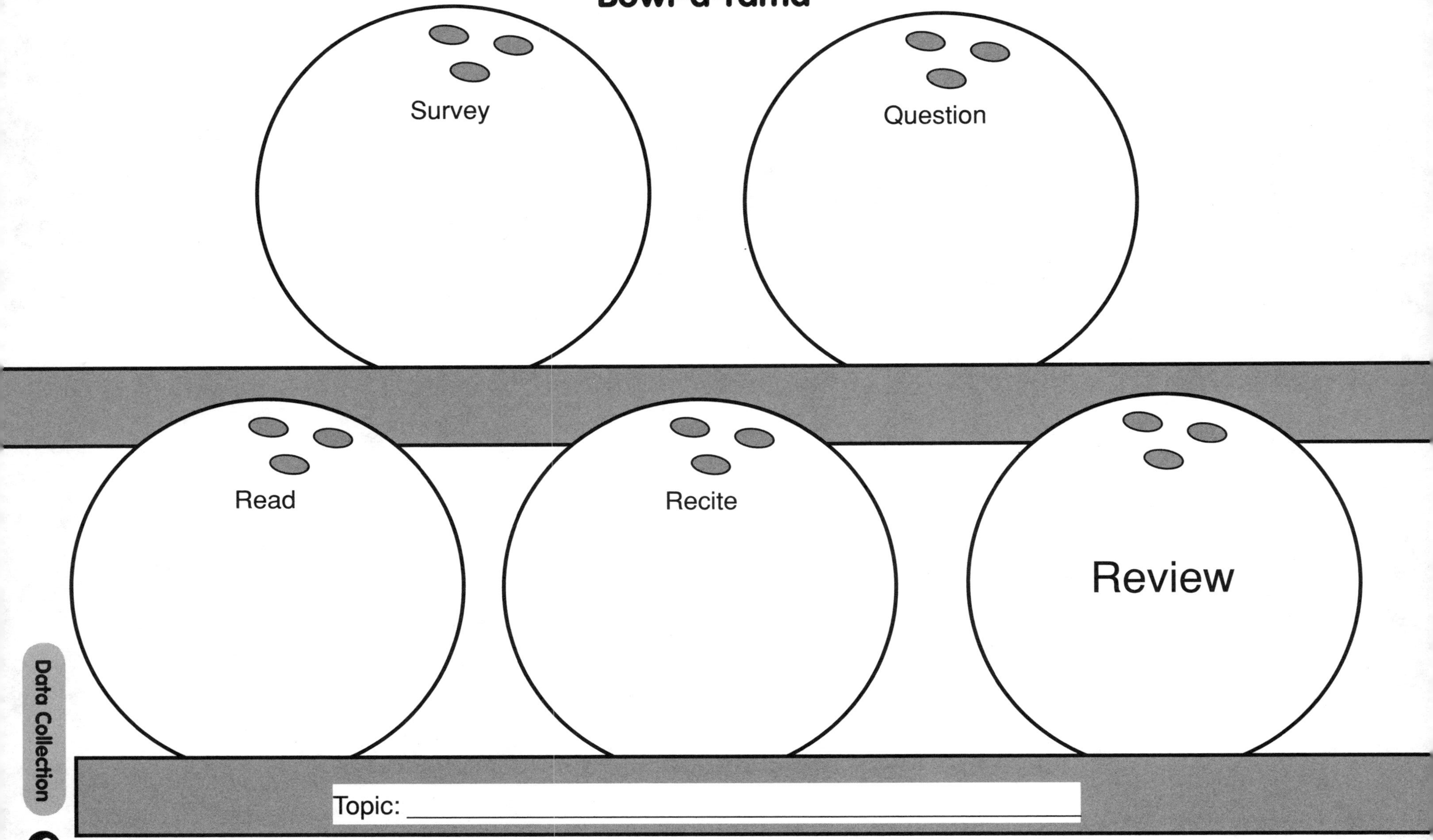

Survey

Review

Recite

Read

Topic: _____

Sweet Sensations

Five-senses chart

Directions for completing page 93:
Record the subject (person, place, or thing) being described. Then write up to four words of your own or from a reading selection that describe each sense related to the subject.

Building Skills

Reading: Have each student use the organizer to **describe the setting of a novel** he is reading.

Writing: Have each student use the organizer to record his thoughts for a descriptive writing activity.

Science: Have student pairs use two copies of the organizer to **compare two different types of trees,** such as a deciduous and an evergreen.

Name

Sweet Sensations

Subject:

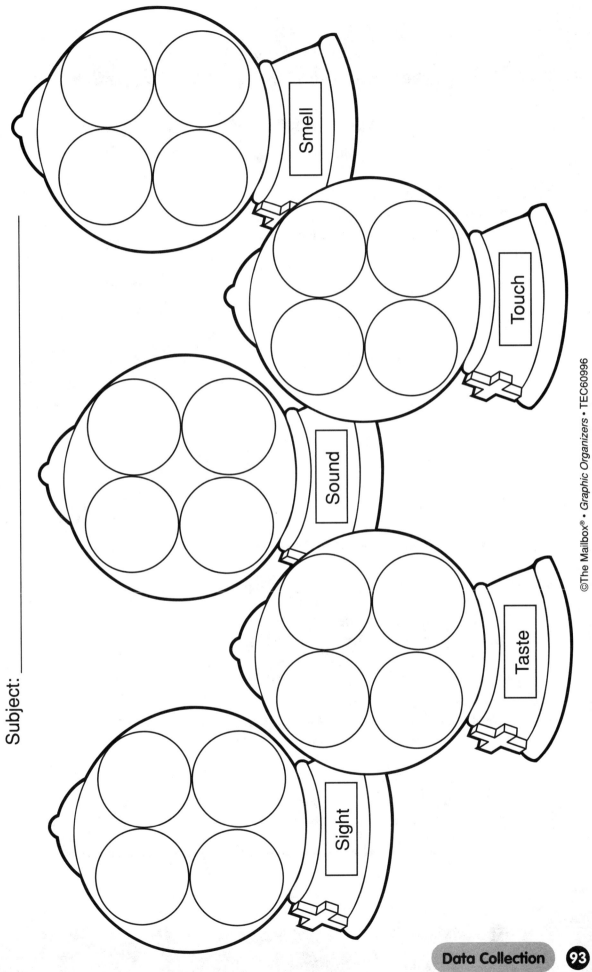

Smell

Touch

Sound

Taste

Sight

Information web

Directions for completing page 95:
Record the topic on the sun. Then record up to eight facts about the topic, writing each fact on a different cloud.

Building Skills

Writing: Have each student use the organizer to plan what she'll include in a ***descriptive-writing assignment.***

Science: Assign each student pair a different topic related to the current unit of study. Then have the partners use the organizer to ***research*** up to eight different facts about the assigned topic.

Social Studies: Have students use the organizer as a way to ***review a particular historical event.***

Name _____

Date _____

Beaming With Information

©The Mailbox® • *Graphic Organizers* • TEC60996

Proud as a Peacock!

Important people web

Directions for completing page 97:

1. Record your name.
2. Record up to 12 names of people who are important to you, such as parents, guardians, siblings, grandparents, scout leaders, teachers, and family friends.
3. Below each name, write how this person is related to you, such as your teacher, scout leader, mother, or father.

Building Skills

Reading: Have students complete the organizer for a **character in a book** they are reading.

Writing: Have each student use the organizer as a prewriting activity for a **personal narrative** about the important people in his life.

Name _____

Date _____

Proud as a Peacock!

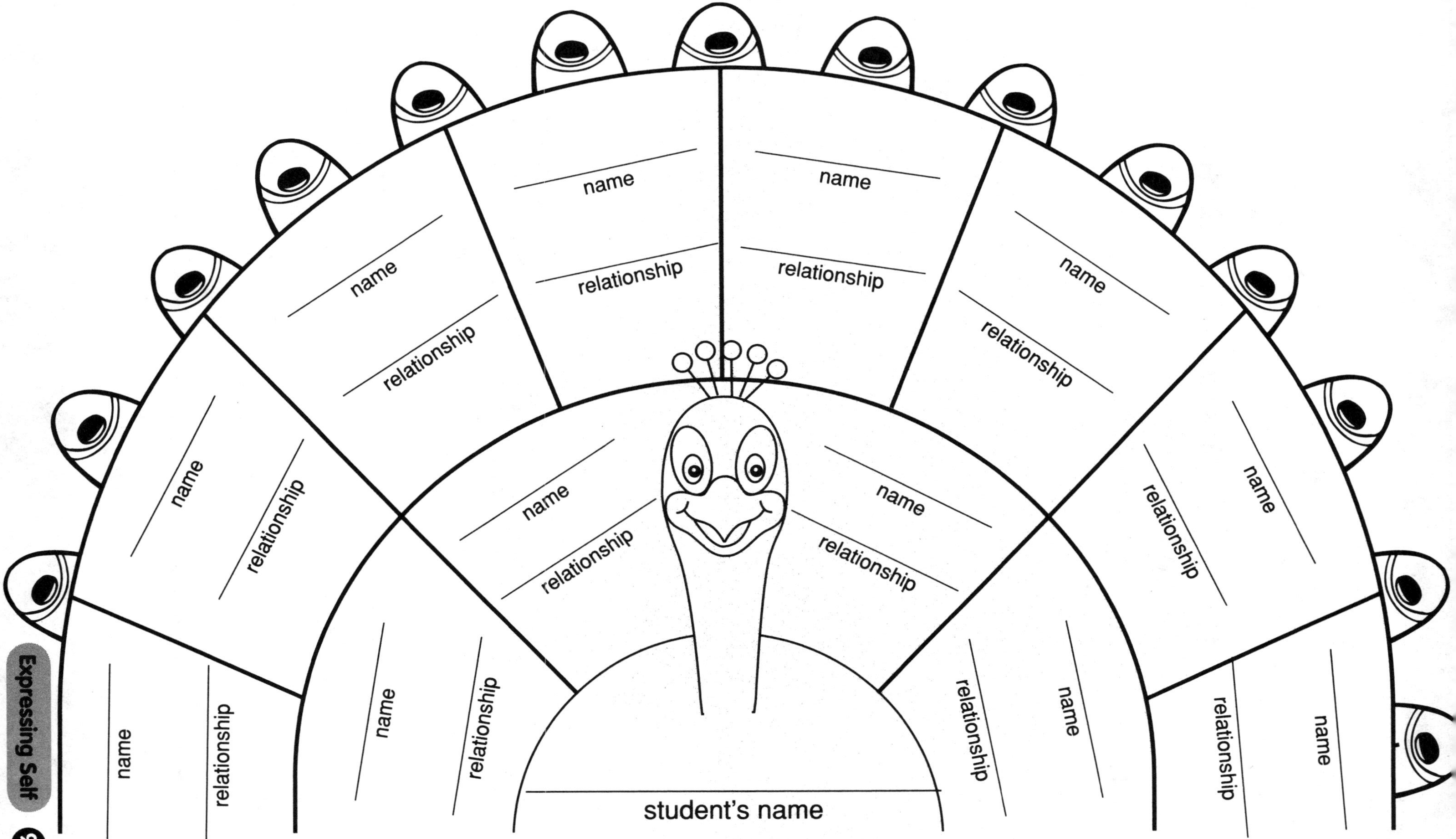

name _____

relationship _____

name _____

relationship _____

name _____

relationship _____

name _____

relationship _____

name _____

relationship _____

name _____

relationship _____

name _____

relationship _____

name _____

relationship _____

name _____

relationship _____

student's name _____

Hear Ye! Hear Ye!

Personal history timeline

Directions for completing page 99:
Record your name. Then, in chronological order beginning with your birth, record the date and a brief description of ten important events in your life.

Hear Ye! Hear Ye!

Building Skills

Writing: Have students use the organizer as a prewriting activity for an **autobiography**.

Writing: After students have completed the organizer as originally intended, provide them with a second organizer. Have each child complete this organizer with **ten future goals** she hopes to achieve.

Social Studies: Have students use the organizer to record the **personal history of a famous person**.

Name_____ Date _____

Hear Ye! Hear Ye!

_____
name

Date: _____
Event: _____

Date: _____
Event: _____

Date: _____
Event: _____

Date: _____
Event: _____

Date: _____
Event: _____

Date: _____
Event: _____

Date: _____
Event: _____

Date: _____
Event: _____

Date: _____
Event: _____

Date: _____
Event: _____

All About Me

Coat of arms

Directions for completing page 101:

1. Record your name.
2. Draw a self-portrait in the space above your name.
3. Complete each labeled section with words and/or pictures.

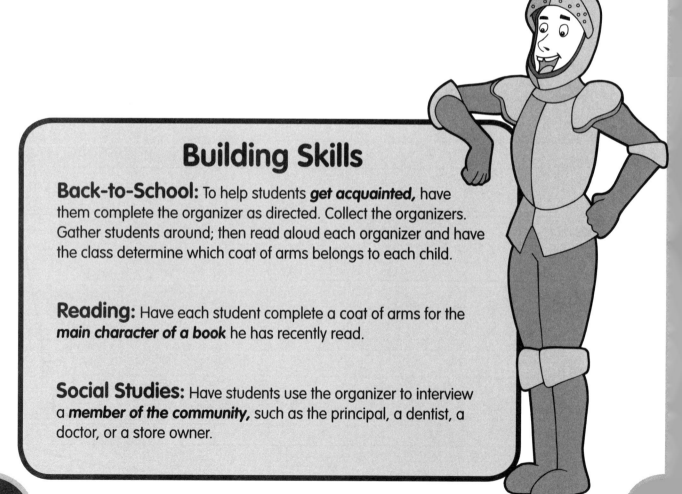

Building Skills

Back-to-School: To help students *get acquainted,* have them complete the organizer as directed. Collect the organizers. Gather students around; then read aloud each organizer and have the class determine which coat of arms belongs to each child.

Reading: Have each student complete a coat of arms for the *main character of a book* he has recently read.

Social Studies: Have students use the organizer to interview a *member of the community,* such as the principal, a dentist, a doctor, or a store owner.

Name _____

Date _____

All About Me

Title: _____

Personality

People Important to Me

Talents/Hobbies

Dreams and Goals

name _____

My Scrapbook Page

Personal-attribute web

Directions for completing page 103:
1. Record your name.
2. Draw a self-portrait in the center circle.
3. Complete each labeled section with words and/or pictures.

Building Skills

Back-to-School: Have students use the organizer to *introduce themselves* to their classmates.

Reading: Guide students in using the organizer to *explore a character* in a chapter book or novel.

Social Studies: Have the student use the organizer to plan a *dramatized introduction of a historical figure.*

Name _____ Date _____

My Scrapbook Page

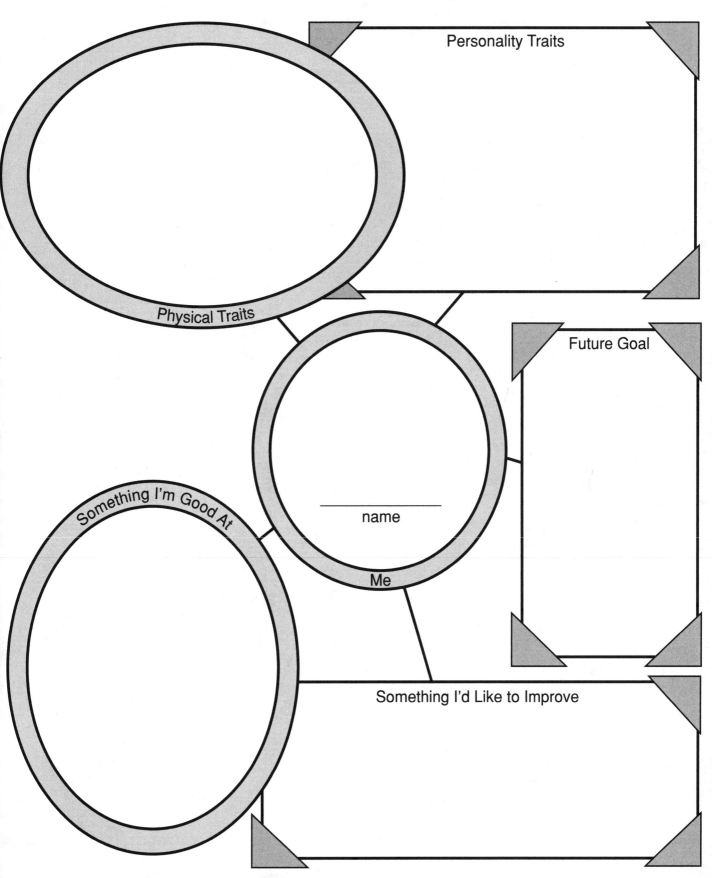

Personality Traits

Physical Traits

Future Goal

Something I'm Good At

_____
name

Me

Something I'd Like to Improve

Solid as a Rock

Decision-making grid

Directions for completing page 105:
Complete Steps 1–6 as directed on the organizer.

Building Skills

Reading: Have students use the organizer to **predict a character's actions** when faced with a decision.

Science: Have each student use the organizer to help her **determine a topic for a science fair presentation.**

Character Education: Use the organizer to help students **make peer decisions.** In advance, program slips of paper with age-appropriate issues, such as one friend not being invited to a party or seeing a good friend cheating. Then give each student pair a programmed slip and a copy of the organizer. Have the partners work together to determine the best decision to make regarding that situation.

Name_____ Date _____

Solid as a Rock

1. Describe a decision that you have to make.

2. List two possible choices for this decision.

3. Consider the first option. List two pros and two cons for this option.
   Pros:
   1.
   2.

   Cons:
   1.
   2.

4. Consider the second option. List two pros and two cons for this option.
   Pros:
   1.
   2.

   Cons:
   1.
   2.

5. Choose the better option. Explain why it is better.

6. Review Steps 2–5. Did you make a good decision? Explain why.

Tunnel Fun!

Problem and solution map

Directions for completing page 107:
1. Describe the problem.
2. Think about how you would like to see the problem solved. Then write your solution.
3. Plan how to achieve that solution. Describe each step of the plan in the spaces provided.
4. Evaluate the process you've described. Is there anything else you would need to do to make sure the problem will be solved? Explain your thoughts in the space provided.

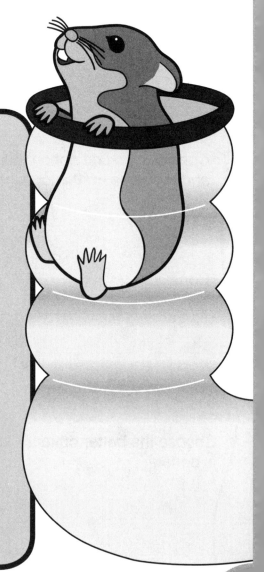

Building Skills

Reading: Ask students to pretend they are facing the **same problem as a book character.** Then have each child complete the organizer by planning his own solution to the problem.

Science: Have students brainstorm a list of **problems or annoyances associated with a modern-day invention,** such as misplacing the TV remote. Then have each child choose one annoyance and use the organizer to plan a solution to the problem.

Social Studies/Writing: Discuss with your students **a problem facing your community,** such as overcrowded schools or not enough parks or recreation areas for kids. Then have each child use the organizer to plan a solution to the problem. Once students have completed their plans, have them use their organizers to write letters to the editor of your local newspaper regarding the problem and suggesting their solutions.

Tunnel Fun!

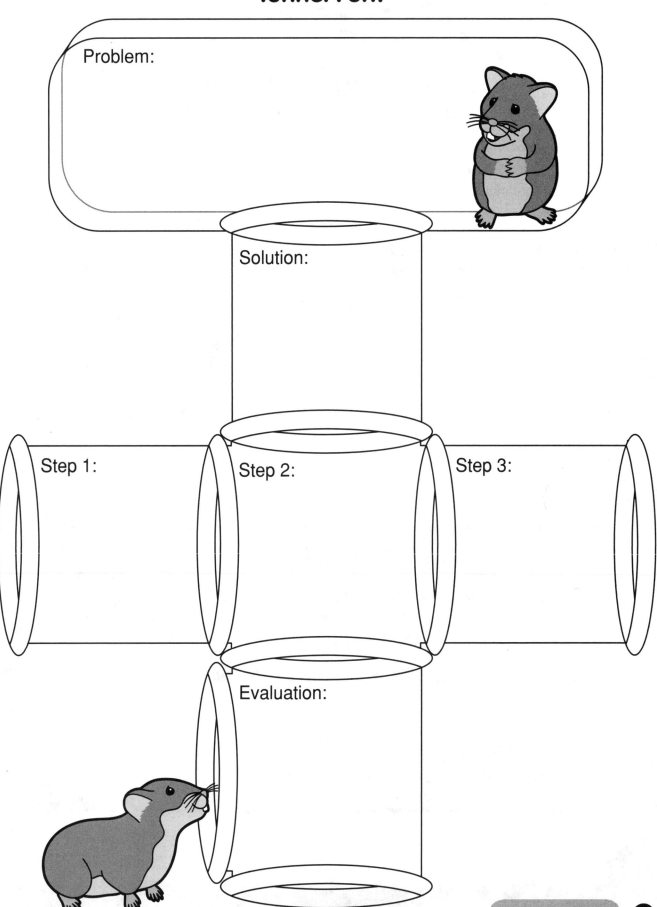

Problem:

Solution:

Step 1:

Step 2:

Step 3:

Evaluation:

Decision Making

Stack It Up!

Project-planning chart

Directions for completing page 109:
1. Record the topic of the project.
2. List the materials needed to complete the project.
3. Record the possible sources from which you'll gather information for the project.
4. Illustrate and/or describe what the project will look like.
5. Create a schedule for completing the project. Then list any additional notes that will be helpful to you.

THIS
END
UP

FRAGILE

Building Skills

Reading: Have each student use the organizer to plan a ***book-talk project***.

Science: Have students use the organizer to plan a ***science fair project***.

Social Studies: Guide each student in using the organizer to plan a ***school or community improvement project***.

Name _____ Date _____

Stack It Up!

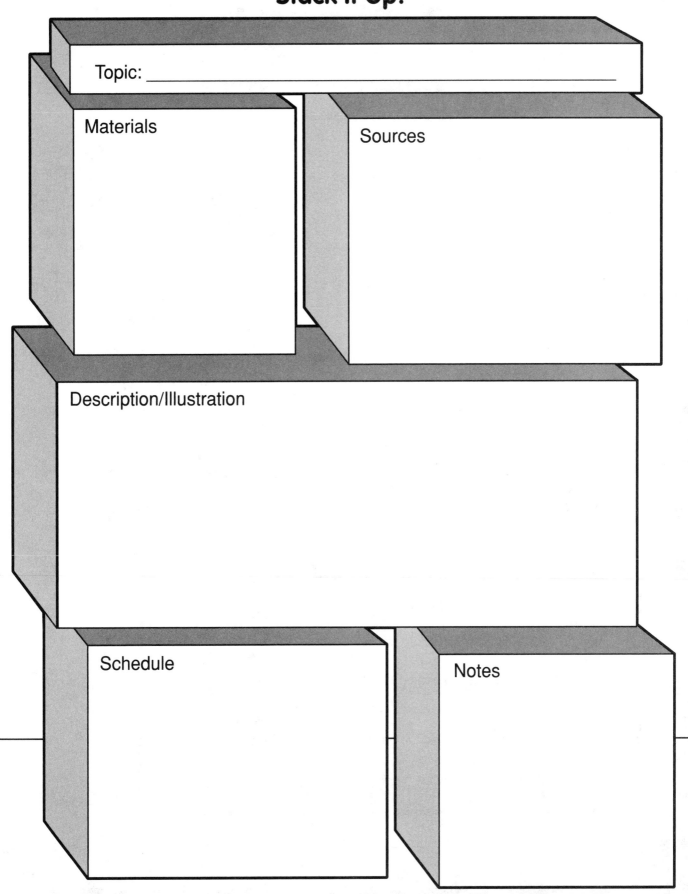

Topic: _____

Materials

Sources

Description/Illustration

Schedule

Notes

Touchdown!

Goal-planning chart

Directions for completing page 111:
Write your goal in the space between the goalposts. Then list in chronological order up to four different actions that you will take to achieve this goal.

Building Skills

Reading: Have each student use the organizer to plan a *reading goal* for the month.

School: Challenge students to use the organizer to plan how to achieve a *study-related goal,* such as improving their grades in a particular subject area or mastering their multiplication tables.

Home: Have students use the organizer to plan how to achieve a *personal goal,* such as earning money for something they want to buy, becoming more physically fit, keeping their rooms clean, or reading more books than the previous year.

Touchdown!

My Goal

4.

3.

2.

1.

_____'s

Homework Log

Monday		_____ date
Tuesday		_____ date
Wednesday		_____ date
Thursday		_____ date
Friday		_____ date

Things to Bring to School:

Other Reminders: